KEY H INDU SCRIPTS

A collection of induction scripts to hypnotize anyone

from

WWW.KEY-HYPNOSIS.COM

Contents

Terms of Use

This collection is supplied under a limited personal license. By purchasing this collection you are buying the personal right to use the scripts in limited ways, you do not own them. You may not distribute the whole or part in any electronic format.

Therapy Use

You may use the scripts in any way you want when working with clients in a face to face situation. You can use them with one client or with a group. You can use them as many times as you want for long as you want.

Education Use

You can print out any of the scripts for classroom use to discuss and analyse in live training sessions provided the www.key-hypnosis.com copyright is acknowledged. You can print out any of the scripts for students to use on other students or volunteers in training sessions. You can print out up to a tenth of the collection as handouts for student materials. You can not distribute any part in any way in electronic format.

Client Recordings

If you use the scripts in therapy and you record your sessions, you can make a recording incorporating the script and give it or sell it to that particular client if that is part of your normal therapy procedure.

Selling Recordings

You may not record any of scripts and then sell the recording commercially or give the recordings away in any media format. You can record scripts for your own personal use for therapy or education.

Distribution

The scripts and other material in the collection are supplied for your personal use only. You may not sell, re-sell, publish, broadcast or give away either the original or copies of all or any part of the collection except as outlined above.

Development

Therapists who use the scripts will find that over time they develop extensions of the original materials or automatically incorporate material from the collection into their own work. You are free to include key-hypnosis.com material in your own work and to do whatever you want with the blended material provided that it does not include more than one quarter of key-hypnosis.com material in it and the copyright is duly acknowledged in any printed material.

INDUCTION SCRIPTS

The scripts in this collection will enable you to put anyone into trance. Everyone can learn to hypnotize, and everyone can be hypnotized. You can learn everything you need to know to do a reliable induction on anyone in about an hour. The induction process usually involves a combination of suggestions, one or more deepeners and one or more tests for depth of trance.

Most published therapy scripts do not include the induction section because each therapist will usually use their one or two favourite induction routines with every client. Some hypnotherapy courses actually only teach one induction, usually Progressive Relaxation or The Elman Induction. These are taught because they are reliable and teachable and do not require any particular skills from the learner. However, they are slow and clumsy and not effective with some people. Therefore every hypnotherapist should learn a variety of inductions, and practice new inductions from time to time. s

Inductions are generally simple. The induction may be preceded by a test for susceptibility and a test for preferred representational style. (Some inductions will need to be re-worded if the client turns out to be unable to visualise, for example). This test can be very simple; just ask '*Can you visualise easily?*'.

There is no advantage in showing off with fancy complicated inductions. Use the simplest induction that will work. The client doesn't know or care how clever your induction is. Often the best induction is no induction. Tell the client to close their eyes and then ask them to imagine they are in their favourite relaxing place and tell them to imagine they are so relaxed they cannot get their eyes to open. Job done – all over in thirty seconds - go straight on with what they came for, the therapy.

Inducing trance is actually very easy. Basically all you have to do is to get the other person to physically relax, and this will open the door to trance; then add a few suggestions anchored to breathing, and most people will go into trance almost immediately. They may well feel that they are fully aware of what is going on but they actually are in trance. This is usually indicated by a change in their breathing pattern, the eyelids flickering, head jerking slightly, fingers twitching or other involuntary physical signs.

Most people will go into trance in less than a minute if you go about it the right way. But, no matter how easy it seems, once the client has their eyes closed you have almost no way to telling if they are really in trance, or just sitting there wondering if they are doing it right and going along with it. You have to test - every time, every client.

The best test is an eye catalepsy test. That lets you know the client is responding to the induction, and lets the client know that they actually are in trance. If there is even the slightest doubt, do a finger lift. Those are very difficult to fake. If you do not get clear evidence then deepen and deepen and test again. Never assume anything, always test. The client is entitled to feel convinced that they actually are in trance. There are few things worse than a client saying afterwards "I don't think I was hypnotised at all. I didn't feel any different".

If you get no response to a depth test ask the client '*What are you experiencing now? Tell me how it seems to you*' and let that guide you. If the client opens their eyes they clearly were not in trance, but this does not mean you have failed or they have failed. All it means is that you need to try a different induction. Ask the client what was going on for them and how they felt and tell them that was really useful information and they are now ready for the second stage and switch to a different induction based on a different induction method. If visualisation didn't get them, then maybe confusion will. If not Confusion, then use Self Induction. If that doesn't work try a physical induction. And so on – everyone can be hypnotised. If people say they can't be, ask them if they have ever dreamed at night. Tell them that is what hypnosis is like and get on with a visual induction. If they say they can't visualize, say to them 'don't visualize a kangaroo'. Ask them 'what came into your mind?', and go on from there.

Remember, the most important ingredient in any induction is the therapist's total unshakeable confidence that it is about to happen. This gets communicated to the client non-verbally. As does any hesitancy or doubt. If you don't think it will work, then that is what will happen.

New hypnotists often ask why we don't just do an instant induction instead of wasting three or four minutes on a relaxation or visualisation induction. The answer is because an instant induction is based on shock, and while it is fine for demonstration or entertainment purposes, many clients are utterly startled by it, and spend the next ten minutes wondering what on earth happened to them and trying desperately to get back in control. This is not how you want your client to be feeling. The gradual induction allows the client to feel in control at all times while your words gently ease them into trance.

About Hypnotic Induction

The scripts in this collection include all the most popular ones, classic inductions, and one or more examples of all the different types there are. There are literally thousands of ways of getting people into trance:

Dissociation Methods

These aim to get the mind to dissociate. Any gentle visualisation will lead the mind away from the present. This is why induction scripts often ask the person to imagine walks in a garden or floating in a bath or rocking gently in a hammock. The mind is then asked to recall or imagine some scene linked to a pleasant situation. When the person is fully immersed in recalling the scene they are in trance. Dissociation and trance are the same thing. Children go into trance almost instantly with this method. In trance sometimes their eyes can be seen to move under their eyelids as they watch the scene suggested by the hypnotist: this shows that they are totally living in their imagination at that moment.

Tonic Immobility Methods

Many animals exhibit a behaviour known as tonic immobility. This is a primitive brain function that causes the animal to 'freeze' as if paralysed. If left unmolested the animal will gradually leave the state and recover normal function. It may be intended to protect the animal from predators by pretending death.

There are many examples in the animal world. It has been known for centuries that chickens can be 'hypnotised' by holding their head down and drawing on a line on the ground straight out from their beak. The chicken can stay immobile for hours. Or the chicken can be immobilised by placing the bird on its back and running your finger from under the beak towards its tail, as if you were gutting it. Some lizards can be 'hypnotised' in much the same way, by tilting them back and stroking their stomach. Some sharks can be immobilised by turning them belly up. The shark appears to lose all ability to swim and lies inert for several minutes before eventually righting itself and swimming away.

Tonic immobility can be induced in humans by startling them. Some will take several minutes to return to full consciousness, others will bounce back from the state almost instantly. This fact is the basis of several instant hypnotic inductions.

A well known method of startling is to tug the arm sharply as part of the induction. Erickson's Handshake Induction is an example of this method.

Sleep Preparation Methods

Chickens put their heads under their wings when going to sleep. They can be briefly 'sent to sleep' by doing that during the day. The chicken will stay that way for thirty seconds or so. This is a case where the physical posture associated with sleep induces the sleep behaviour. Humans also exhibit this behaviour. If you get a human to sit or lie quietly, relax their muscles and slow their breathing they will invoke the natural human sleep response. This is why most inductions start with 'take a deep breath and relax' – it starts the natural sleep response.

Sensory Overload Methods

These work by overloading the mind. This prevents analytical clients from 'over-thinking' and evaluating everything you say. You can use confusion methods by rapidly switching the subject around and confusing the mind until it gives up trying, or you can just make the client monitor more and more sensations until they can't handle any more and it becomes easier to just focus your instructions.

Imitation Methods

These are based on the natural human mental response called 'mirroring'. If you see someone else do something part of your mind rehearses the same actions. If you watch someone getting ready to throw a ball, neurons in your brain prepare you to do the same thing and create the muscle commands ready to fire off. Hypnotists use this ability to induce trance. If you get the client to describe what they would do to put someone else in trance, they are in fact rehearsing it in their own mind first, and of course it starts to work on them as they are describing it. Erickson's My Friend John Induction is an example of this method

Metaphor methods

This is a huge class of methods. Almost anything can be used that metaphorically suggests the ideas of sleep preparation: down, dark, quiet, calm, relaxed. So watching a sunset and linking things getting darker and quieter as the sun goes down to breathing will work, or going down in a lift, or going down stairs or imagining being a bird circling down towards a dark silent sea will do it. The Deep Blue Induction and the Swirling Paper Induction uses this method.

Monotony methods

Many inductions actually depend on boring the listener until their mind drifts away in self defence. A lot of meditation inductions depend on this technique: meaningless phrases spaced out with long gaps in between. Any school kid can tell you how easy it is to drift into a daydream while the teacher drones on about something you are not interested in.

Guide to the scripts layout

Each script is laid out in four columns. The first column shows the target of the hypnotic technique being used. The second column gives the wording of the suggestion. The third column has a code that indicates what type of suggestion is being used. The fourth column has notes and explanations of how the particular line of the script works.

Meaning of the codes used in column three:

I	Indirect Suggestion	
D	Direct Suggestion	
K	Kinesthetic reaction	aiming at a muscular memory reaction
A	Auditory reaction	encouraging an auditory recall
M	Metaphor reaction	using a metaphor
V	Visualization reaction	encouraging a visualization
=	Equivalence	Doing one thing is the same as another thing
/	Opposite	The more of one thing the less of the other thing
>	Cause and Effect	Doing one thing causes the other thing

Beginners Inductions

The Basic Induction: How to Hypnotize Someone

This script is a simple fairly full proof induction for the absolute beginner. It will put almost anyone into trance. It is a good induction for the beginner to try.

It is useful to have ready as a hand out for public talks about hypnosis. If you are doing demonstrations to a group, get them to work in pairs, give out this script and invite them to hypnotize each other.

Steps	You say to the person...
Step 1	*start with relaxing the muscles*
	Settle yourself down now... as you begin to relax...
remove any tension	shrug your shoulders and let them go... lift your arms slightly and then drop them down... rotate your head... ease out any tension from your neck... your back... tense your leg muscles and then let them relax...
permission	That's right...
Step 2	*then talk about their breathing*
begin the relaxation	Now take a deep breath... and just let it out... now another deep breath,... and as you let it out... allow yourself to relax even more... and then one more breath... and really let your yourself relax...
permission	That's good....
Step 3	*tell them to focus attention on one thing*
Suggestion breathing = relaxing	now become aware of your breathing... of how your breath is moving gently in and out... as you relax... and then become aware of ... how on every breath out ... you can relax a little more... and just tell yourself that with every gentle breath out... relaxing deeper and deeper...
	and take a few moments now to relax even more... deeply... completely... and notice how that relaxation progresses... smoothly...
Step 4	*get them to close their eyes*
	... and become aware that as you are thinking about going deeper and deeper you can become even more comfortable... and how nice it is to just close your eyes and drift away...

	whenever you want to...
Step 5	*make them even more relaxed*
	... and I wonder if you can imagine a quiet, peaceful spot... maybe on a warm afternoon... to imagine lying comfortably... somewhere nice... somewhere you can relax ... calm and peaceful... mind drifting away... imagine your arms and legs... are beginning to feel tired and heavy... as heavy as lead... to relax ... totally... to just let things go... and drift away...
Step 6	*take them deeper...*
	..and imagine being in a room somewhere,... and in that room there are stairs going down... and you can go down those stairs... safe and secure ... warm and comfortable... carried gently down and down... more deeply relaxed... and with each step your body relaxes more... and your mind relaxes more...
Countdown Induction	and there are ten steps going down... and you can go down those steps now ... going deeper and deeper with every comfortable breath... 10... 9 ... more and more relaxed... 8 ... more comfortable... 7... and 6... deeper and deeper... and as you go down each step down you are feeling more and more comfortable... 5.... and 4... and 3... and by and by you are drifting off into an endless velvety welcoming dreamland...
Step 7	*test they are in trance*
	... and now focus your attention on your eyes... those eyes can become so relaxed, so tired that you just cannot open them, it is as if those eyes are glued tight shut.
	And I'd like you now to pretend that those eyes are so relaxed... so tired... that you just cannot open them... it is as if those eyes are glued tight shut... and they just won't work...
	And when you are sure that have relaxed those eyes to the point where you just cannot open them... and they just don't work...
	You can try to open them... and you will find that they just won't work... it's as if those eyes are glued tight shut... and they just don't work.
	[tries to open the eyes... failure means they are in hypnosis now]
Step 8	*deepen the hypnosis again*
	That's good... that's exactly the way it should be...
	I wonder if you can imagine being in a comfortable chair...

	just relaxing somewhere... breathing gently... and going into a pleasant dreamy feeling... letting your mind drift away... nothing to do ... you don't have think... you don't have to do anything at all... except enjoy that lovely feeling... nothing bothers you... calm and relaxed...
	That's good... and just allow your mind to relax even more...
Step 8	*here is where you put the hypnotic suggestions*
Step 9	And while you are in this state your mind is open to many possibilities... you can imagine things vividly... you can recall feelings and memories... you can become aware of things in your mind... and things in your body... and outside your body... as if you are floating... weightless... and open to all experiences...
	Now become aware of you hands... allow your mind to think about the feeling in your hands... the weight... the temperature... the way they are lying... and while you are more and more aware of your hands... you can become aware that some part of you mind feels a need to move some part of your hand... a finger or a thumb... and you can just allow that to happen... do not assist in any way... just allow it to happen on its own... and it may start as a tiny tremor... you might feel a tingle or it might be something else... allow that movement to be, and then we can go on...
	[wait for a response, you should see a tiny movement. If it is a big, immediate lift of a finger, then the person is faking it. Tell them to open their eyes and talk to you about what they felt].
	[If you get a tiny movement then they are in trance. You can then give whatever suggestions you want to. 99% of people will be hypnotized by this stage.]
Step 10	*Bring them out*
	And now it's time to return to the present. I am now going to count from five up to one, and when I get to one... you will be back in the present... awake and alert and ready for the rest of your day. 5... 4... 3... 2... ONE.

David Mason   www.key-hypnosis.com © 2009

Dr. Flowers Hypnotherapy Script
A simple but effective hypnosis induction Script

This simple induction combines fractionation and relaxation and countdown induction methods to put someone into trance. It starts by encouraging dissociation, then muscular relaxation, then paces and leads with suggestions tied to eye movements.

This type of induction has come to be known as The Doctor Flowers induction. It has the advantage over the Elman Induction of being quicker and simpler, and you don't have to touch the client. It is also a good induction to use when you are hypnotizing a group of people.

	Dr. Flowers Hypnosis Induction		
Capability	I am going to show you how you can go into hypnosis. I am fairly sure that you have the type of mind that goes into trance quickly and easily.	I	Priming expectation
	So just settle yourself down there... and we'll begin the process	>	Seeding relaxation
	Are you ready to go into trance?		Expectation
	Good, that's right...		Reassurance
	Now, this is how you go into trance.	I	Bind
	I am going to count some numbers, and as I count you are going to open and close your eyes until you get the feeling that you just can't open them again.		
	OK with that?		bind
	Now let's just practice. You can look at the back of your hand, or someplace in front of you... I am going to say 1,2,3 and after I say one, you close your eyes briefly, and then open them again. Then at two you close your eyes briefly and then open them again. Got that? Good... here goes...		
	One		
	Two		
	Three		
	Excellent. You are doing it just right.		Reassurance
	Now, this is where you put yourself into trance.		Bind
	I am going to count out loud, and I want you to		

close your eyes after each number, and then re-open them. But this time, as you close your eyes, I want you to roll your eyes up behind your eyelids, as if you are looking at a point in the middle of your forehead. OK?		
And when your eyes are rolled up looking that point in the middle of your forehead... I want you to breathe out, and as you breathe out... let yourself relax... feel your body relaxing...	K	
so we'll do that now... ONE... close your eyes... and breathe out...		
That's right... and as you open your eyes... become aware of how your eyelids are feeling heavy...	K	
And again... TWO... roll the eyes up... relax the body... imagine those eyelids getting heavier...		
and THREE... breathing out.. relaxing... eyes getting heavier...		Pace with breathing
and FOUR...		
FIVE...		
SIX.. and those eyes are getting heavier now... and at some point those eyes will not want to open...		
SEVEN... and when you feel that relaxation...		
EIGHT... you can leave the eyes closed... and focus on relaxing more with each breath...		
and as each number gets bigger, those eyes are getting heavier... and harder to open...		
[Keep counting until the eyes are closed and the breathing is steady and the body shows signs of relaxation].		
and now feel those eyes closing down... feel those eyelids heavy and relaxed... so relaxed that you can't open them...	I	
and keep on breathing and relaxing until you are sure that you just can't open them..	I	
and then when you try to open them... they will get twice as heavy... twice as relaxed...	D	
That's right,,, and just enjoy that lovely relaxed feeling...and let it spread to the rest of your	K	Eye catalepsy

	body... and when you are really relaxed.. you can try to open them... and the more you try the harder they stay locked shut... that's right...	test

David Mason   www.key-hypnosis.com © 2011

Classic Inductions

The Elman Induction

Procedure: The Elman Induction was popularised by the American stage hypnotist Dave Elman. He needed an induction that would always work, even when used by inexperienced people. He developed it as a way of teaching hypnosis to doctors and dentists who had no background in hypnosis and needed something easy to remember that could be followed from a script. It still used a lot even though it is over fifty years old. There are hundreds of variants of the basic format.

Method: The procedure works by using a scattergun approach: using multiple induction techniques one after the other. It goes through four techniques: muscle relaxation; fractionation; countdown; and shock induction, with constant deepening.

Advantages: It is actually slow but it has the advantage of being reliable and easy to learn. It helps the learner by giving a fixed procedure to follow and trains the novice in what to look for due to its repeated tests for indicators of trance.

Disadvantages: Slow and cumbersome. The main problem with this induction is that clients often keep going with the numbers. If the client does not stop after a few, they probably are not in trance at all, and you need to switch smoothly to another induction as if that is exactly the way it is supposed to go.

	The Setup		
	[this whole section is an echo of the old fashioned authoritarian style… you will do what I say!]	I	
Capability	Now in a moment I am going to show you how to go into trance... how to relax your body and your mind... in a really good way that you will enjoy...		
Behaviour	and once you start on that process no power on earth can stop you going into trance	=	
Capability	and you don't have to do anything... it will just happen... as long as you follow my instructions you will go into trance easily and swiftly...	>	

	Relax the body		
	So now... just settle back and relax yourself... take a deep breath and then just let it go... that's right...		
	Now take another breath and feel your eyes closing down... and as your eyes are closing let your body relax...	D	Large muscle relaxation
	shrug your shoulders... let your arms and hands go loose and limp and floppy... that's right...	D	
	and as you are relaxing you can move your attention to your eyes. Just become aware of those eyes, and the little muscles that control your eyelids... and those eyes can become so relaxed that you just cannot open them... and as long as you keep that relaxation there... those eyelids will become so relaxed... that you just cannot open them...		small muscle relaxation
	and when you know you have relaxed those eyes and you know they will not open you can try to open them... and you will find that they just won't work...		TEST: Eye catalepsy
	That's right... you can try but they just don't work... so you can stop testing now... and just enjoy that feeling of relaxation getting deeper and deeper...		Reassurance
	And now become aware of the quality of that relaxation... and imagine that relaxation spreading through the whole of your body... sweeping down from the top of your head to the tips of your toes... like a wave of relaxation... letting go... let go and relax every muscle, every nerve, every fibre of your body... that's right...	D	
	and feel yourself drifting deeper and deeper as that happens...	D	Deepener
	And now you can deepen this feeling even more...	D	Fractionation
	Fractionation		
	And as deep are you are now... you can go ten times deeper. In a moment I am going to ask	>	

	you to open your eyes... and then when you close them you will go ten times deeper in trance...	
	Now you may find it difficult to open your eyes... but you should be able to open them a bit... so try opening them a bit now... and then allow them to close and go ten times deeper... that's right that's good.	D TEST: Compliance
	And as relaxed as you are now... you can actually become ten times more relaxed... so when you are ready you can try to open your eyes a second time and you might be able to open them a little and then as those eyelids come down you feel yourself going ten times deeper again...	D
	And try it for a third time... and as those eyes shut tight... you will go even deeper... ten times deeper...	
Arm Drop		
	Allow yourself to get comfortable and totally relax your body.... In a moment I am going to lift your arm... do not assist in any way... just let your arm be loose and limp...	
	[lift one arm by the wrist... gently waggle the arm... it should be soft and pliable... this is test of depth of relaxation]	TEST: physical relaxation
	And in a moment I am going to release your arm and as it drops down you will go even deeper into trance... *[let go the arm and it flops down, causing a momentary shock, or you can pull the arm and then drop it]* That's right... allow yourself to go deeper down now...	Simple shock induction
Countdown		
	And now it is time to relax your mind... I want you shortly to start counting aloud quietly... counting from 100 down to as far as you can go... and as you count... after each number you will say to yourself... think to yourself... 'Deeper and Deeper'... 'Deeper and Deeper'... and as you say each number and feel yourself go deeper and deeper... you will notice that it becomes harder and harder to remember the	D

	next number... and your mind becomes more relaxed... more at ease... until you just cannot remember the next number...		
	And you can relax those numbers right out of your mind... and as you do so... you will go deeper still ... into a lovely state of easy relaxation...	>	
	So starting now... I will count with you to start with... 100... deeper and deeper... 99 deeper and deeper... 98 deeper and deeper... and as you count those numbers will relax you more and more... just allow those numbers to take you deeper and deeper...	>	
	And when you have relaxed those numbers right out of your mind... you can stop counting....	I	Bind: 'when'
	And when the last number has disappeared you can signal by moving a finger or thumb and we will go on... when you are ready...		TEST: finger signal
	[Carry on with the therapy]		

Dave Mason © 2009 www.key-hypnosis.com

Progressive Muscle Relaxation Induction

Hypnotic relaxation induction

The progressive relaxation induction is the easiest hypnotic induction. The progressive relaxation hypnosis is simple and reliable, and every hypnotist should know how to use this induction.

Progressive relaxation induction is also called the Jacobson relaxation method. The basic technique (PMR) is to tense and then relax each muscle group, progressing from the head to the feet, while suggesting deeper relaxation.

Progressive relaxation script is quick to learn and will work with everyone, but sometimes can take a long time to induce trance. With the progressive relaxation induction it can be difficult to tell when to stop the induction. Learning the progressive relaxation induction is good practice for beginners, but there are better inductions.

Relax the body, relax the mind

	PRE TALK SECTION		
	I would like you to sit down or lie down and make yourself as comfortable as you can...		
	loosen any tight clothes... take off your shoes if you want... take anything bulky out of your pockets so that you can relax easily		
	please make sure your cell phone has gone into trance already...		Metaphor
	I am going to speak to you about relaxation... about comfort... so your mind can drift off to... enjoy a new experience...		seeding ideas
	Hypnosis is safe and pleasant and at all times part of you will be in trance and some part of you will be aware of what is going on... and you will be able to come out of trance any time you want to .... the feeling of trance is a lovely relaxed peacefulness... you will feel as if you could do anything... but you just can't be bothered... you would rather relax and enjoy the experience...		reassurance = you have control
	everything I say will be intended for your own good, and anything I mistakenly might say that might not be, you can just ignore it and let it go by...		Safety

	If at any time you want to move to make yourself even more comfortable... you can do that... you are in control...	**D** reassurance
	I am going to ask you to close your eyes, and while you are going into trance I will be touching you on one or both wrists...	Bind
	is that OK?	Permission to proceed
	[get agreement]	

BREATHING INDUCTION SECTION

	Allow yourself to settle down comfortably now... and when you are comfortable... think about being supported... when you become aware of how the chair is touching your back... just allow your eyes to close.	Permissive Bind
Breath 1	Now take a deep breath and hold it ... and when you let it out ... slowly... just let your body relax... that's right... just relax as far as you are comfortable...	Use the natural parasympath-etic response
Breath 2	And now take another deep breath... and this time when you release it ... just release all the tension in your body... just allow yourself to relax completely...	
Breath 3	And when you are ready... take another deep breath... and this time really let go... let go any remaining tension...	
Metaphor	Allow your arms and legs and hands and head to go limp and loose and floppy... just like a rag doll... or imagine an old coat thrown across a chair...	**V** Visualization
Capability	And as relaxed as you are now... you may be surprised to learn that you can be even more relaxed... deeper and deeper relaxed... ten times more relaxed... even more...	**I** presupposition

FIRST PROGRESSIVE MUSCLE RELAXATION

Eyes	Now focus your attention on your eyes... on those tiny muscles that close your eyelids... and you can control those muscles... I wonder if you can imagine them so relaxed that they will just not work...	**I**

Head	and when you are sure that those eyes are so relaxed that they won't work then allow that relaxation to spread to the muscles of your forehead... feel those muscles spreading out and flattening... feel some relaxation spread to your cheeks... feel them relax and flatten... then allow that relaxation to go down into your jaw... allow your jaw and mouth and lips to relax... allow your whole face to relax... to smooth out...	dissociation
	[*You should see some movement of the mouth or jaw if they are following your suggestion*] That's right... your jaw and mouth and head are all becoming so relaxed... you are doing very well...	progressive relaxation
Shoulders	and now allow that relaxation to spread to your neck and shoulders... just pull your shoulders up a fraction if you can... and then relax them totally... let them fall as far as they will go... just imagine all those muscles flattening and stretching... imagine every nerve and fiber becoming loose and limp and heavy... just feel that weight pulling your shoulders down until they are just lying there completely relaxed and comfortable.	sensory distortion
Chest	Now imagine all the muscles of your chest relaxing... imagine all those muscles that connect to your spine and tummy... imagine how much they can relax... and let them relax now... and with each gentle breath you can relax those muscles more and more... [*Safety: Do not mention the heart at all, ever*]	Continue the progressive muscle relaxation downwards
Arms	and your arms... become aware of how relaxed your arms might become... and you can gently tense your upper arms a little... and then let it go... and that letting go allows you relax that part even more... and then maybe you can tense your forearms a little... and let that go... and notice how much more relaxation can flow into those arms... and then check if those hands need to relax... you can gently softly tense your hands... or even	Dissociation

	just imagine you can tense your hands... and let go again... and your hands are totally relaxed... and you can forget all about your heavy hands and arms and just enjoy feeling wonderfully relaxed...		
	PROGRESSIVE MUSCLE RELAXATION DEPTH TEST		
Arm Flop Test	And in a moment I am going to lift your right hand by the wrist... you can continue to relax and go deeper and deeper... you don't have to pay any attention at all to what I do... do not try to assist... you can just let it happen... as if it is somebody else's arm... just let the arm go soft and limp and bendy... when I lift your arm it will be so relaxed it will just flop like a wet towel...	**D**	Depth test
	Lifting your arm now... *[always warn before you touch the listener]*		
	[Take the wrist between your thumb and forefinger and lift it straight up. Try to hold it by the bony knobs of the lower arm, not the upper part of the hand. The arm should feel heavy, and it should bend at the elbow, not the shoulder. If you waggle the wrist the hand should flop around. If the whole arm comes up quickly and there is no weight, then the person is assisting and is not yet in trance.]		Test for complete muscle relaxation
Arm flop deepener	In a moment I am going to let your wrist go... and when that arm falls you will feel yourself going even deeper into relaxation... could be ten times more relaxed than you are now... feeling warm and safe and comfortable as you go deeper...		
	NOW... *[let the wrist go, ...do not place it down gently, let it drop]*		
	[In a fully hypnotized person the arm will drop like a dead weight. Otherwise the listener is not in trance and so you then start another round of relaxing using the legs. Very occasionally a person's arm will stay up when you let go. This means the person is		

	actually already in a deep state of hypnosis, the best you can get. Tell them to allow their arm to drift slowly down and wait until it has.]		
	[If you are sure your person is trance then...] That's right... and as I speak to you my words will allow you to go as deep and relaxed as you want... You are doing very well. Thank you... and now we will move on [*now do whatever you plan to do next*]		
SECOND MUSCLE RELAXATION DEEPENER			
	[If the person is not in hypnosis or you are not sure then do the second arm drop and go on to do the Second Relaxation.]		
Second Arm Drop	In a moment I am going to lift your left hand by the wrist... you can continue to relax and go deeper and deeper... once again you don't have to pay any attention at all to what I do... just let it happen... as if that arm was somebody else's... just let the arm be soft and utterly relaxed... when I lift your arm it will be so relaxed it will just flop like a wet towel...	I	Supposition
	Lifting your left wrist now... *[always warn before you touch the listener]*		
	[This time give the wrist a little tug as you lift it and drop it immediately. The whole arm should move a little. The idea is to give a tiny surprise, something unexpected that will briefly shock the listener out of their current state.]		
	[Then say immediately, while the arm is falling... Firmly, and in a deeper voice] DEEPER NOW... DOWN AND DOWN.	D	
	That's right. You can allow yourself to let go now... really let go and go deeper and deeper now... relax every muscle in your body... and maybe you can feel a wave of relaxation flowing down your body... from your head down... all the way down to your toes...	D	Continue the suggestions of progressive muscle relaxation
	... and the more you relax... the easier it	>	

	becomes to relax even more...		
	SECOND PROGRESSIVE MUSCLE RELAXATION		
	And I wonder if you can imagine your legs now... how the bones and muscles are all connected... and maybe you can imagine those big strong muscles in your upper legs... and really feel where they are and how they work together... and those legs can feel really heavy... your whole body can feel really heavy...	**D**	Dissociation
Upper legs	and you can lightly tense the muscles at the front maybe... and then at the back and the side... and then you can release and relax ... and feel those muscles go soft... and maybe you can see in your mind's eye those muscles sliding past each other... to go to rest... and those legs can get so heavy... so relaxed, can't they?	**D**	Progressive muscle relaxation of the lower body
Lower legs	and you can move your attention to the muscles of your lower leg... and gently, gently tense and release those muscles too... and every time you release you might be able to sense the relaxation that's happening all through your body as each part learns to really let go now...		
Feet	and your feet... they can relax too... you might want to gently tense first one foot and then the other and you might have difficulty deciding which foot to think about first... and it might all seem too much trouble... and as you do you imagine those feet relaxing... all tension gone...		
Inward focus	and it might feel as if those feet have gone too... relaxation can make it seem as though those feet are very far away... as if they are not really connected to you at all any more... and you can lose touch with your legs maybe... being so relaxed lets you focus inward...		Dissociation
	People can just drift away when they are relaxed... when nothing matters... the mind		Dissociation

	just drifts where it will... as if it has forgotten all about arms and legs and just enjoy that feeling of drifting weightless...	
	SECOND MUSCLE RELAXATION DEPTH TEST	
	And when people are really relaxed they can forget about everything nearly... nothing seems important... it can be hard to summon up the energy to do anything... it's just so pleasant to relax...	D
Ideomotor depth test	I would like you to become aware of your hands... and you can become aware that there is a difference between your hands... and I don't know what that difference is ... but you will know... one hand may feel heavier than the other, or one hand may feel warmer, or one hand may start tingling... you can sense a difference of some kind now or maybe later... and I would like you to allow your unconscious mind to choose one hand... and I don't know how the mind will know... but just let the unconscious mind decide on a hand... don't try to choose or assist in any way... just let it happen naturally... and you can be curious as to which hand it will be... and when your mind has chosen one hand I would like you to signal by raising a finger or a thumb of that hand, to show that the hand has been chosen... so in your own time, now, let your mind choose one hand or the other, and signal by raising a finger or a thumb or maybe the whole hand will move... just let it happen... and we will move on...	
ideomotor signal	*[Await movement: you may have to wait two or three minutes if the person is deep in trance. When the signal comes it should be a small, hesitant movement. If the movement is immediate and strong, like one finger juts up straight away fully rigid, your person is not in trance so you then start another round of deepening and relaxation. (If there is no movement at all then the person may be so*	

	deeply in trance that they have lost control of their muscles. They think they have signaled, but nothing moves. Test by doing an arm drop. If it is totally limp they are in trance.)]		
	[*If you get a small movement or do the arm drop say...*] Thank you. I see your signal. That's very good. You are doing very well... We will move on now... [*and go on to whatever you decide to do next*]		
	[If you get a clear signal then you are done, otherwise go on to the third section *(I told you this could take a while).*]		
THIRD PROGRESSIVE MUSCLE RELAXATION			
	Thank you. That's very good. I see your signal. And as you are lying there, relaxed, breathing gently, listening to my voice... part of you may be wondering if you are going into trance while another part of you is already in trance.		
	What I would like you to do now is to mentally go round every part of your body... and just check if there is any tension there... your shoulders, your arms, your legs... and if there is focus on that part... imagine it... imagine how it would feel if it was totally relaxed... completely at ease... imagine with every breath out that there is a voice in your head talking to that part... What would it say? What words or thoughts or pictures or sounds would really make each part relax totally?		Allow the person to hypnotize themself
Capability	And you can take as much time as you want to visit every part of your body... test and relax it... until you are totally relaxed all over... and maybe you will be surprised at how easy it is... and maybe you actually are already relaxed all over... and some part of you didn't recognize it... because everybody can relax... you can relax... you can give permission now for every part of you to experience that wonderful feeling that really relaxing brings...	D	Truism

Second ideomotor signal	And so in your own way and in your own time... relax that body... and when you have done that... let your mind surprise you by choosing a hand to signal with to show you are totally relaxed and ready to move on...		
	[Await the signal. If you do not get the right signal you have been very unlucky with the person you picked to work with. You can either give up and choose another person, or start the whole process from the top. It will work, eventually. Using the progressive muscle relaxation script you usually get definite, testable trance in less than ten minutes.]		

Dave Mason © 2008 www.key-hypnosis.com

How to use the script

The relaxation hypnosis script does not need any special voice control or emphasis. Just say the suggestions in your normal voice, as if you were talking to a child. Try not to read the script... you can refer to it as much as you want... but don't read from it directly if you can avoid it. The exact words are not important, the continuous gentle flow of suggestions is.

The script needs to be delivered slowly... very gently and slowly... suggesting rather than commanding... pausing briefly at each ellipsis ("...") and trying to match your pace to the pace of the listener's breathing. Watch the listener closely all the time. If they make any movement, comment on it, and say 'Yes, that's right, that's exactly right' so they get feedback and approval and reassurance.

Try to time each statement or group of statements with the out-breath of the listener. You cannot deliver it too slowly - leave the listener lots of time to think about and then act on your suggestions. It might seem incredibly slow to you, but it does not seem slow to your listener. There is nothing wrong with stopping and saying nothing for thirty or forty seconds, to allow the listener time to feel the changes taking place inside them. Silence is the best deepener. Remember that the listener has been told to keep on relaxing and going deeper, so they will use the silences as suggestions to do that.

Eye Fixation Induction

Description: The Eye Fixation Induction is very old and not particularly useful.

Method: It is a pace and lead induction. When it works, it works by using the fact that eyes staring at a point will quickly get tired, and the eye naturally starts to defocus. The hypnotist paces this and suggests that it is happening because of the suggestions. But many clients notice their eyes defocusing and drifting, know they were told to stare at the point, and so actively start to control their eyes, which takes them right out of trance and into heightened alertness. All the hypnotist can do is keep going and hope they will eventually get bored and shut their eyes. Not a good choice.

Disadvantages: It is taught as a simple induction to beginners, but in fact it is hard to get right. It works well with highly susceptible people, but it does not work at all with people who are in the least bit sceptical. That type of client is left with their eyes wide open staring at a wall, trying to see non-existent changes and all the while their mind is actively disputing what is being said to them by the hypnotist.

Uses: Many hypnotists use this as their standard induction, but there are better and more reliable inductions around.

Extensions: It can be fun to use at a dinner party: get a friend to stare at a candle flame, and suggest that as the flame flickers their eyes are getting tired and want to close. Then tell them their eyes are locked shut and you have a great party stunt.

	The Setup		
	Just make yourself comfortable now... get into a position where you can relax... and look at that wall in front of you...	I	Seeding comfort, relaxation
	lift your eyes up until you are looking up, higher than your normal eye level...		Strain the eye muscles
	and now let your eyes find something on that wall... some spot or corner or maybe a small object... and let your eyes rest on that ... and just look at that spot or that point... for a few moments	I	
	just keep focusing on that spot...		
	[pause]		
	The Induction		
	and while keeping your focus on that spot... become aware of the muscles around your eyes...		Dissocation

	how they they are holding your eyes up... and your eyelids... and what they feel like...		
	and as you look at that spot you might see that it begins to waver... or maybe you see it blurring ... or that image might start to get a sort of halo round it...	D	Pacing experience
	and you might notice that those muscles are becoming tired... and as you think about those muscles... they are becoming more tired... and you might need to blink... and that's OK	D	Pace with blinking
	And you might wonder if that blink is slower than normal... and you might might like to think about how nice it would be to allow your eyes and eyelids to relax... and close those tired eyes...	D	Pace with blinking
	and that is telling you that your eyes are getting tired and ready to close... and when you are ready... when your eyes are so tired and heavy you can just let them close on their own...	>	
	and it can be so good and relaxing to close those eyes... and closing those eyes means you can relax now... really let yourself relax...	D	
	deep... deeply, deeply relax...	D	look for eyelid trembling
	That's right...		
	[Carry on with the therapy]		

Dave Mason © 2009 www.key-hypnosis.com

My Friend John Induction

Description: The My Friend John Induction is a powerful hypnotic induction. This induction is attributed to Erickson.

Method: It is actually a self induction, the listener pretends to be a hypnotist by following everything the hypnotist says. But the process of repeating the hypnotic instructions puts the hypnotic ideas into the listener's mind and causes them to go into trance.

Advantages: It is simple and flexible - ideal for the client who is very analytical or is suspicious of hypnotism and afraid of losing control.

Uses: It is often used if a standard technique is not working. It is particularly effective with teenagers, who often think they are too smart to be taken in by hypnosis, don't like authority and will resist direct inductions.

	The Setup		
	Maybe you are curious about hypnosis and maybe you wonder how it works and wondering how well it might work with you?	I	Mind reading
	It's natural to be curious about something like that and before you even think about being hypnotised I would like to explain to you how I put other people into trance. Is that OK?	I	Bind
	[get confirmation]		
	It's probably easiest if you imagine you were hypnotising someone else. So just listen to me describe how I would do it. You don't have to anything except listen.		
	The Induction		
	Just imagine there is someone sitting in that chair beside you, or in another chair somewhere, or even lying down...	D	Visualis-ation
	And what you do is... you tell them gently to relax... say to them... Relax... let your shoulders droop.... let your arms flop... imagine how the arms could just lie heavy and relaxed... as if they were made of lead...	D	
	And then tell them... let your legs relax now... just allow you legs and feet to be so relaxed that they	D	

	feel heavy and totally relaxed now...		
	In your mind... say to them... focus on your breathing... now... and with each breath out... you can find yourself... relaxing more and more... and each gentle breath will take them deeper and deeper... more and more relaxed...	D	Breathing induction
	just focus on each breath... and allow each breath to make those arms and legs... more relaxed... and wonder how relaxed a person could get...	I	
	And in your mind imagine what it would feel for them to be so relaxed that they could hardly keep their eyes open... imagine them relaxing... head sinking comfortably... imagine how their eyes could be so tired that every blink gets longer... and the eyes stay shut longer... and what it might like to close those eyes... think what it would be like to feel your eyelids getting heavier and heavier and how nice it would be to allow them to shut and relax too...		them: ambiguity
	and then imagine saying to the person... focus on the little muscles around your eyes... the tiny weak little muscles that control your eyelids... and what would it be like to pretend that those eyelids were so relaxed that they just won't work.... if those eyelids were so relaxed, so at ease that they just cannot open...		look for eyelid trembling
	And say... focus your awareness on those eyes... and how it feels when those eyes just will not open... when it feels as if they are locked tight shut... and just will not work...		Look for eye movements
	Tell them to imagine going down... and I don't know... you might like to think of a staircase... or a ramp... or an elevator going down... or something else... that you can say imagine going down and down... and with each breath you go down further and deeper... and count down silently with each breath... from ten to one... and as each number passes go deeper and deeper... more at ease... more comfortable...		Staircase deepener
	[pause]		
	And now... allow the mind to focus on the hands... allow the mind to become aware of the left hand		Depth test

and the right hand... what they are feeling... where they are... and allow the mind to choose one hand or the other hand and you might become curious as to which hand will be chosen... and when the mind has chosen...		
One finger or a thumb will lift on its own... entirely without effort... or it might be a hand or a wrist or something else... and that will a signal that you have done what you want...	Look for confirmation of trance	
[Carry on with the therapy]		

Dave Mason © 2009 www.key-hypnosis.com

Erickson Handshake Induction

Description: The Handshake Induction is an instant induction developed by Milton Erickson, the famous hypnotist. When done properly it seems like magic. It is a perfect example of how to hypnotize someone instantly.

Procedure: You approach someone and offer to shake hands, and but instead do something unexpected. This hypnotism technique causes their subconscious mind to be overwhelmed, and to accept your command to go into hypnosis.

Advantages: Good for demonstrations, often used in stage hypnosis.

Disadvantages: It requires total confidence and a fluid continuous delivery. You only have a few seconds to grab their attention and do the induction.

Uses: It is normally used for hypnotizing a client unexpectedly, as a demonstration of hypnotic mind control by a stage hypnotist.

Extensions: Once you understand the basics of a pattern interrupt hypnotic induction you will learn to do endless variations on it and how to hypnotize people anywhere.

HANDSHAKE INDUCTION

	The Setup		
	The handshake induction is a pattern interrupt induction. We all prefer to do things in a predictable way. Once you have learned a routine it becomes automatic and we stop thinking about how to do it. This frees the brain to go on and do other things. For example, when you are driving, you see a red light and your foot automatically moves to the brake pedal. You don't think about it, it is so automatic that many people sometimes do it when they are front seat passengers and not even driving.		
	You can take advantage of patterns like these. When you start a behaviour pattern that is automatic your mind expects the pattern to continue and stops paying attention to it. Once started, the behaviour goes on 'automatic pilot'.		
	However, if anything occurs to interrupt the sequence of actions, then your mind has to stop what it is doing,		

	and focus on the set of actions that has suddenly gone wrong.		
	If at the same time, while the mind is puzzling over what went wrong, another pattern is started then the mind has to switch to paying attention to that, leaving one set of behaviors hanging.		
	If the second set of actions is unusual and unexpected then the mind is divided between thinking about completing the original set of actions and thinking about the unexpected set of actions.		
	This causes a temporary, very temporary, overload of the cognitive function. In the few seconds that the mind is in this state, it can be hijacked.		
	Any sudden word or movement will cause the mind to go into a defensive state. In that state the mind will obey whatever instructions it gets, since it wants to do something, but is confused.		
	The Induction		
	The handshake induction is almost all physical, there are very few words used.		
	You approach someone you want to put into trance. They should not be expecting the induction. Erickson was fond of doing it to people who declared publicly in his presence that they couldn't be hypnotized. He then dropped them into trance like a stone.		
	As they get near you put out your right hand as if to meet them with a handshake.		
	This starts the pattern. If someone approached you with their right hand out and a smile, you naturally put your hand out and initiate the handshaking routine that you done thousands of times before.		
	As you get right up to them, and their right hand is out ready to be shaken, you drop your right hand, and your left hand comes up and grabs their right wrist.		
	This interrupts the pattern. Suddenly things are not going as they were expected to. Their brain goes into overdrive trying to work out what is going on.		
	As you grab their right wrist, in one continuous fluid motion, you lift their right hand right up in front of their face.		
	This produces a threat. Their mind is thrown off		

balance for a second or two by the startling event.		
You then turn the palm of their hand toward their face.		
You then either look into their eyes and then at the hand quizzically, as if to say 'there's something odd here' or you can say 'Well?' as if expecting some sort of answer.		
This causes them to be confused. You will see their eyes kind of unfocus as their mind goes inward to make sense of this strange happening.		
At that point you do something sudden, loud or dramatic. The intention is to startle them into a confusion induction.		
The moment you see their eyes glaze you either jerk the hand, or shout 'SLEEP!' or do something else unexpected.		
Be ready to put your arm around them to support them, in case they lose the power of their legs and begin to crumple.		
You immediately start talking. Say something like... 'You are safe. Just allow your mind to relax and go deeper. Deeper and deeper. Your legs will support you. And you can allow your mind to let go and relax now... deeper and deeper... deeper asleep... so relaxed and comfortable... safe and warm and comfortable as your mind goes in deep deep relaxation....'		
You must start talking immediately after you deliver the startle command. You have only two or three seconds before the person's mind starts taking back control and they start to demand 'what the hell do you think you are doing?'.		
However, if you speak immediately then most people will drop instantly in trance, and you can continue with whatever you want to do next.		
It is a very satisfying and showy induction.		

Dave Mason © 2009 www.key-hypnosis.com

The Sensory Overload Induction

Description: The Sensory Overload Induction is a classic distraction induction. The person's attention is focused on evaluating sensory inputs to the exclusion of all else.

Procedure: It is relatively easy to do. Just use whatever is happening around them and get the client to focus on each input as it occurs, without giving them time to deal with any one sensation before moving on. Keep piling on more sensations for them to monitor.

Method: It works because it gets over the analytical person's tendency to critically examine every word and suggestion by giving them too many things to think about to keep track of them all, and so their mind just gives up trying and accepts whatever you say.

Advantage: It is particularly useful with analytic or hypervigilant clients who can otherwise be difficult to get into trance.

Disadvantage: won't work in a totally silent room.

Uses: Analytical clients

	Keep adding more and more sensations...		
	Just settle into the chair, and get comfortable.. I am going to be talking about various things and you might want to keep track of them... or you might not... it's up to you... to let go when you want	I	Permission to be in control
	so settle back and settle down... and you can close your eyes... anytime you want to ...	I	
	And I'd like you to listen to the sound of my voice and the sound of the words that I am using... and maybe think about the shapes of the words...		Thinking about analyzing words
	and as you do become aware of the other sounds around... the sounds from within the building... out in the street... the sounds coming from inside you... and the sounds of my words as they are rising and falling, changing...		Overload with sounds
	and these sounds can be so interesting and you can find them relaxing you... and the only sound you need to listen to as you hear the other sounds is the sound of my voice...	>	
	and that sound can make you want to relax and	>	

	settle even more... and you can find yourself going deeper into the chair as you relax to the words...	V	
	and as you relax deeper listening to all those sounds you can become aware of your body in the chair the feel of the chair on your back and the weight of your legs and how your arms are lying relaxed on the arms the arms can get as heavy as the legs are getting heavy... and under your hands your fingers can become aware without moving of the texture of the material and how that texture is similar to and different from the feeling of heavy arms and legs	V	Overload with feeling from the body
	and you might feel that weight increasing as you lie there thinking about the texture of the sounds and shape of the words and the colour of the weight gently pressing down now... as you relax	V	Synesthesia
	and become aware of the feeling of your feet on the floor... and they can begin to become numb and heavy... as you are aware of the sounds and words and relaxing arms and heavy legs... and other parts becoming heavy now just relax	V	Overload with proprioception
	and focus on your breathing and aware of how your breath is allowing to relax more and more to let go and go deeper and deeper as relax into the chair now... your shoulder loosening as your feet go numb and the sounds go round and the weight is relaxing and going down...	D	Overload by focus on breathing
Memory	and those gentle steady breaths can remind you of how you can ignore everything as you settle down to sleep to let go and allow your mind to drift away... dreamy drifty floating... like a dream taking over and enjoying the feeling of release... calm...	V	Reminder of going to sleep
	and everything settling more comfortably now like something is finally settled and using those sounds to become even more relaxed... imagine going down deeper and deeper...	V	
	nothing to think about... nothing to do... except drifting down and enjoying the feeling... how	I	

	easily you let go when you want to go...		
	and feel your whole body becoming away of that body it's shape and size and weight and position as you focus on your breathing it can feel like you are drifting away from it...	D	Dissociation
	Soft and gentle and relaxed... feeling everything relaxing and softening loosening more and more enjoying the release... and now aware that your face is relaxed... your jaw is relaxing... thinking or not thinking aware of all the tension is gone completely	D	
	and down relaxed released not thinking not knowing not caring every muscle relaxed feeling so good... so calm... know you could ... but can't be bothered...		Mind reading
	And everything lets go... goes down until there is only being and not being... floating and drifting... so nice to just let go...		Dissociation
	[either do another deepener, or carry on with the therapy]		

Dave Mason © 2009 www.key-hypnosis.com

Swinging Watch Hypnosis induction

An old fashioned but effective hypnosis induction Script

This is one of the earliest hypnosis inductions. Any time hypnosis is mentioned in movies a swinging watch is used to hypnotize the person.

The swinging watch induction has gone out style since people stopped wearing gold pocket watches. The swinging watch induction works well on most people, especially if they are expecting to get hypnotized with a swinging watch. You don't actually need a swinging watch. Any kind of pendulum object will do. As you see signs of the person going into trance, pace and lead them and link every change to going deeper and deeper...

	Hypnosis Induction		
Capability	I wonder if you are the kind of person who goes into hypnosis easily?... Most people are... especially those who think they won't be.	D	Priming
Capability	I am fairly sure that you have the type of mind that goes into trance quickly and easily.	I	Creating expectation
	So just settle yourself down there... and we'll begin the process	>	Seeding relaxation
	Are you ready to try something new?		Expectation
	Good, that's right...		Reassurance
Behaviour	Now, as long as you know how to relax you can go into trance.	I	Bind
	I am going to hold up my watch... and I want you to look at it... and I want to you keep your eyes on the watch... follow it with your eyes... never take your eyes off the watch...		
	Do you think you can do that?		bind
	[Hold out the watch on the end of the chain at a comfortable distance from their face... and start to swing the watch slowly from side to side in front of them...]		
	Now I want you focus your attention on the watch...		Leading
	Watch the watch as it swings from side to		Leading

side...		
Do not take your eyes from the watch...		Leading
Excellent. You are doing it just right.		Reassurance
Now, as you focus on the watch... as you follow the watch... your eyes are getting tired and heavy...	D	Bind
and each time the watch swings past your eyes... those eyes are getting heavy and tired... tired and heavy...		
And the sound of my voice is making you more tired... making your eyes more tired... your eyes are growing heavier with every word you hear...		
and following the watch with your eyes... your eyes are getting more and more tired... more and more ready to close...	>	
and as that watch swings across you are finding it harder and harder to keep your eyes open now... and those eyes are growing heavier ... so heavy...		Pace with breathing
and you become aware of how your eyelids are feeling heavy... so heavy... so heavy that they just want to close... your whole body wants to relax... is relaxing ... deeper and deeper now...	D	
those eyelids getting heavier... and you just have to close your eyes now...	D	
and your body is relaxing... eyes getting heavier... eyes closing	D	
and it is so nice to close those eyes... and as you enjoy that feeling... the whole of body is starting to relax now... letting go...		
[keep swinging the watch and let your voice get slower and deeper...]		
and as your body is relaxing your mind is relaxing ... and those eyes are so relaxed that you can't open them...	>	Pacing
and keep on breathing and relaxing until you are sure that you just can't open them..	I	Bind
and then when you try to open them... those eyes get twice as heavy... and your body goes twice as relaxed... and you just cannot open	D	Eye catalepsy test

	those eyes.		
	That's right... and now stop trying... and just enjoy that lovely relaxed feeling...and let it spread to the rest of your body... that's right...		Trance achieved.

David Mason © 2011 www.key-hypnosis.com

Countdown Inductions

Countdown Induction

Target	Induction section		Technique
	Before you begin going into your hypnotic trance now just make yourself comfortable. Just settle yourself down and you can relax now. All you have to do is to focus on becoming comfortable.	D	Bind
	Take a moment now and wiggle about until you are in the right position for what comes next.	I	lack of Reference
	Look around your body and notice if there is any tightness, or any discomfort, and maybe just shrug everything until you are happily settled down and ready. If anything is making you uncomfortable then fix it.		
	Fixing things stops them bothering you doesn't it?		Truism
	Now, in a moment I am going to count down from ten to one, and when I get to one you will have relaxed into a deep satisfying trance. But before that you can move every part of your body as you become loose and floppy and relaxed.		
	Now take a deep breath and relax it. Just let it all flow out... ahhhhh. That's right. Now tense up your whole body, and then let go again... really relax... and feel how good that is...		Progressive relaxation induction
	TEN... focus your attention on your feet ... think about your feet... think about letting your feet and toes and ankles relax and get loose.		
	NINE... Now relax all the muscles in your legs... in you calves, your knees your thighs... very relaxed... feel those legs getting heavy and heavier...		
	EIGHT... now feel that relaxation spreading into your body... your chest....		
	SEVEN... and now feel that relaxation in your shoulders... spreading all the way down your arms... down to you hands... your fingers... and those arms feel so heavy... so relaxed... it is as if they belong to someone else...		
	SIX... and now allow your neck to relax... and		

	become aware of your face relaxing... your cheeks... your jaw... your lips ...	
	FIVE... let your eyes relax... your eyebrows...your forehead...	
	FOUR... and everything feels loose and heavy... as if you arms and legs were made of stone... totally relaxed... you can feel the weight pressing down... and you just can't move those arms and legs now... and you can enjoy this feeling of total relaxation... letting go... and the more you relax the more you can relax...	
	THREE... and as your mind drifts off you feel a wave of relaxation travelling down your body ... down and down... from the top of your head... relaxing your face... relaxing your neck... your shoulders your body... spreading... down and down... gently and easily... feel your body sinking down... safe and warm and secure...	
	TWO... and each soft gentle breath out... is relaxing you more... and that relaxing means you can relax deeper and deeper now... letting go... drifting away... nothing matters... enjoying that that lovely feeling...	
	ONE... and totally relaxed now... totally at ease... and your mind can drift away to a place... far, far away.... a place where you feel relaxed... where you feel comfortable... always... and think of what the place is like... what other places there might be that you make you feel comfortable... maybe a beach at twilight... or a favourite chair... or snuggled warm in bed on a stormy night... or maybe floating in warm water... allow your mind to drift over these things and other things... whatever feels right for you... as you drift ever deeper... enjoying the feeling ... nothing matters... nothing is important... just being in the moment... let your mind empty...	Dissociation

Dave Mason © 2009 www.key-hypnosis.com

The Staircase Inductions

The staircase induction is probably the most used formal hypnosis induction technique. It is simple and flexible and there are endless variations of it. The staircase metaphor can be used as a hypnosis induction or a hypnotic deepener. Here are two typical staircase hypnosis induction scripts that show how the technique is used.

For an unusual variation on it, see the My Friend John Induction

Staircase Induction

	Suggestions		
	And I wonder if you can imagine a big old house somewhere?....		dissociation
	... with a fence... and a big garden... and maybe there are trees...		Gives time to think
	... it's the sort of house that families grew up in... generations of people... living and laughing....		engage personal experience
Memory	There's been weddings and parties... Christmas trees and Easter Eggs... and birthday candles and happy times...	I	engage visualisation
	...inside that house... there's a staircase...		
	And you can find yourself at the top of that staircase...	I	
	...and I don't know if that staircase is wood or marble... or carpet... doesn't matter....		all alternatives
	...and there can be a handrail...		safety
	...and you can imagine yourself beginning to go down those steps... safe and secure... comfortable... because at the bottom there is a door...		
	... and behind that door is a wonderful thing, for you.		anticipation, safety
	... and you can begin to go down those steps now ... and with every step you get more relaxed... and deeper into trance	D	standard staircase deepener
	and so TEN going down... deeper relaxed... and NINE deeper still....	D	
	... and EIGHT... deeper relaxed...	D	

..and SEVEN... down and down...	D	
.. and SIX...		
And feel yourself sinking into that chair... wonderfully supported as if you are lying on a fleecy cloud... just allowing yourself to drift....	D	dissociation
...and FIVE... deeper and deeper....		
...and FOUR ... down and down...	D	
... and THREE...		
...and TWO...		
...and there is one step left...		
... and when you go down from that last step... there is just zero...and you can imagine drifting through the centre of that zero... through a black void of nothingness... a wonderful soft velvety warm comfortable darkness... you are relaxed and at ease... your mind is completely relaxed...	D	
...and the only thing of importance is the sound of my voice... everything else can fade away...	D	
[Now do a depth test, for example asking what colour the door is]		

Spiral Stair induction

Here is another example of the stairs induction, this time using a spiral staircase. This is particularly effective with children. It can be combined with a confusion induction and used to create trance in highly analytic clients.

	DISSOCIATION DEEPENER		
	And I wonder if you can feel yourself sinking gently into that chair, now... and feeling yourself supported as if you are on a big fleecy cloud... and just drifting down and down...into that cloud... feeling yourself going deeper and deeper... deeper and deeper...	I	Sensory
	Just allowing yourself to drift away now... nothing is important... nothing matters... and you can feel yourself going down and down..	D	Supposition
	And my voice can become whatever you want it be... my voice can become the sound of rain on the window pane on a winter's night... or my voice can be the voice of a teacher... or a parent... or a friend... and my voice can be the wind blowing along an empty street... in summer... or maybe... the wind is blowing along a street in autumn...		Dissociation
	And picks up a leaf and that leaf gets carried away ... here and there... and it goes left and right... and up and down... and that wind... carries the leaf safely and gently... as it goes round and round... swirling and swooping...		Confusion
	And then it goes down... gently ... swirling round... as if it is in a spiral stair case...		
	And I wonder if you can imagine a spiral staircase... the way the spiral staircase goes down and round and round... and you can imagine yourself on that spiral staircase... and you can imagine going down that spiral staircase... and there can be a handrail and it's safe...		Visualisation
	And you can count yourself down that spiral staircase... and the first step is TEN... and the next step goes down deeper NINE... and EIGHT feeling more relaxed and more		Countdown Pace with breathing

	comfortable... and SEVEN drifting away... then SIX down and down.... really relax... then FIVE deeper and deeper... and then FOUR... nothing matters... nothing counts... you have nothing to do... you don't have to do anything... you don't have to think... listen... anything at all... and then THREE nearing the bottom... totally relaxed... then TWO ... almost there ... and ONE... gone down... into some warm dark place... where your mind can just drift away...		
	if any thoughts come into your mind just let them go... like little puppies running away wagging their tails... you can ignore them... they'll just go away...		
	and then ONE... you're at the bottom... feeling really good... totally relaxed...		
Behaviour	and you can just enjoy that feeling of release and relaxation... knowing that everything's OK and you're OK... and there are no issues... nothing you have to do...		
	That's very good... you're doing very well...		Reassurance
	[Now do a depth test]		

Escalator induction

Hypnotic inductions do not have to be long or clever. It is easy to put most people into trance. This induction is a simple conversational induction with a minimal deepener. It uses the idea of a continuous escalator, instead of a countdown as the deepener.

	The client should be sitting quietly...		
	And it's odd for me to think of you sitting there now... just breathing gently... wondering about... how easily... how quickly... you can go into that lovely relaxed state...		Ambiguity - I who is 'wondering'?
	and while wondering... maybe you can imagine		My Friend

someone just like you... some other person wanting to go into that relaxed dreamy state... and how you could help that person into that state of comfort... of quiet relaxation... and you might imagine saying to that person... become aware of your breathing... of how your breath moves gently in and out... and tell them... how on every breath out ... you can relax a little more... and just rest for a few moments... and allow time to relax... deeply... completely... and notice how that relaxation progresses... smoothly...	John induction
... and then get them to imagine a quiet, peaceful spot... maybe on a warm afternoon... to imagine lying comfortably... somewhere nice... mind drifting away... imagine arms and legs... eyelids... are beginning to feel tired and heavy... as heavy as lead... to relax ... totally... to just let things go... and drift away...	
...and now imagine being at the top of an escalator... a moving staircase... looking down... and allow them to be carried down that escalator... safely and securely... carried gently down and down... more deeply relaxed... as that escalator goes down.. carried deeper and deeper... the body relaxes more... and your mind relaxes more... going deeper and deeper with every comfortable breath... and by and by you are drifting off into an endless velvety welcoming dreamland...	Deepener
[and now do a depth test]	

Dave Mason © 2009 www.key-hypnosis.com

Double the Numbers Induction

The Double the Numbers Induction is a variation on the staircase or escalator induction.

Principle: Using numbers is fine, but most people have difficulty not linking their counting to their breathing. This induction gets over that difficulty by giving the listener a line to follow. The listener then strings the numbers at different points along the line and relaxes more as they pass each number.

Use: It is particularly useful as a self induction.

Advantage: The advantage of this type of induction is that it allows the listener to relax at their own pace, and is gentler and more client focused than the standard 'one to ten' countdown induction.

Disadvantages: needs to be able to visualise the line.

Extensions: This type of induction can be adapted to anything linear - a ladder, fishing line, telephone lines etc.

Target	The induction - Relax the body...		Technique
	Take a deep breath... and let it go...		Slow down
	Now take another deep breath... and as you breathe out... just allow your whole body to relax and go limp....		the breathing
	and on the next breath... allow your eyes to close...		eye closure
	Now become aware of your body... notice if there is any tension anywhere... try shrugging your shoulders and letting them drop.... tense your legs and let them relax... roll your neck and let it relax... anywhere that is not loose... just tense and relax... until your whole body feels loose and heavy... and allow that feeling to continue.		Physical relaxation
	First Deepener - count down		
memory	And now I want you to imagine a line... or a chain or something like that... and I want you to imagine the numbers one to ten are spaced out along that line... and I want you to make the distance between number two and number three double the distance between one and two... and the distance between three and four is twice the distance of the distance between two and three...	V	Always offer a choice of possible ways to form the line.

	and so on... each number is separated by twice the distance of the previous number...		
Capability	And just imagine going along that line... from one to two... and two to three... and three to four... and the distances between each number gets longer and longer...		
	And as you think about that line... just imagine that in your mind you are sliding along the line... and as each number passes you get more relaxed... more at ease... and you can just feel yourself sinking ... down and down... and just keep doing that... and your breathing will get slower... and your pulse will get deeper....	I	
	And as each number comes along it gives you more time to relax... to let go...		
	and when you reach ten... you can just allow yourself to drift down and down some more... deeper and deeper... more and more relaxed... down and down...	>	
	allow that feeling to develop... you don't have to think... you don't have to do anything... all you have to do is to enjoy that lovely feeling of deep, deep relaxation...	I	
	and you can forget about everything... just allow your mind to drift away...	D	
	and if any day to day thoughts come into your mind... that's OK... you can just stack them off to one side... and deal with them later... they're not important... nothing is important now...	D	
	... and each breath out is taking you deeper and deeper now... more and more relaxed...	>	breathing deepener

Lazy Numbers Induction

The Lazy Numbers induction script is a variation of the normal Disappearing Numbers Hypnotic Induction. The standard Wipe-out-the-numbers induction tells the client to make the numbers disappear but does not give any instructions as to how they should do that. This induction treats the numbers as animated things that can get tired and relax and fall asleep.

It is a fun way of playing around with the standard method. This script shows that there is no end to the ways you can put someone into trance.

	Lazy Numbers Induction script		
	So settle back now, get comfortable... and close your eyes...		
Relax the body	Now take a deep breath, and hold it... and ... just let it all go... ahhhh... That's good...		Start releasing tension
	When you are ready... take another deep breath.... and as you do... lift your shoulders up... and as you breath out... let them slump down and relax.		Let go muscle tension
	And I wonder if you would relax more...		Bind
Visualisation	by thinking about lying on a beach somewhere... or maybe remembering relaxing in a garden, some green place... or somewhere else that you really can relax in...	V	Dissociation
	and while you relax deeper and deeper...		Bind
	Think about a big blue sky... the sky on a lovely day... just the sort of day you like...	V	Dissociation
	and imagine now in that sky... a cloud... and when you look at a cloud... it sometimes seems to be a shape... that reminds you of something...	M	Dissociation
TEN	and just imagine that this cloud changes into the number ten... and it can be a one and zero... or it could be ten little clouds or some other way that that cloud reminds you of the	V	

	number ten... and then as you breathe out... just watch as that number dissolves... disappears like steam... and as it disappears you can feel all the tension in you disappear... getting more and more relaxed...		
NINE	and the number nine appears... a fluffy... soft... cloudy... number nine... and then on the next breath out allow that number nine to gently fall over... as if it is too tired to stay up right any more... and as it lies there it sags and flattens out and you can feel yourself relaxing more now too... lazy and letting go...	M	
EIGHT	just relaxing as the number eight comes... and that eight is so relaxed... too relaxed to stay together and the two circles separate and gently fall down and they roll away as you relax deeper now...	M	
SEVEN	and then think of seven... and that seven unbends... loses all its tension.. straightens out... flops down... and lies flat... and gently sinking down...	V	
SIX	a six appears... and this six slowly falls over and lies on its back rocking gently.. then uncurls... lying out flat... and loose an limp... until it is so spread out it just isn't there... letting go... relaxing now ... relaxing more and more as you let go of each number...	V	
FIVE	and five... the five is like a soft little blow up toy... and letting go all the air inside... it begins to deflate... getting soft and squishy and wrinkled... and gets smaller and smaller ... going down and down... until it too disappears...	M	
FOUR	now four... the four is tired and lazy and relaxed... and the four just slumps down... like a sand timer running down... or dog sleeping in the afternoon heat... softly lying down... lying there relaxed and calm and quiet...	M	
THREE	and three is like three soft balls of wool... hard to know where one ends... strands of	M	

	wool weaving soft fabric like down and down as that soft fluffy number gets all mixed up and you can't tell where things begin or end... and it really doesn't matter now...		
TWO	and then two... too relaxed to care... too relaxed to think now... and everything just too easy to let go		
ONE	and two merges into one and one doesn't have to think or do anything...		
	just relaxing... no one idea or two much to care... and drifting away like soft cotton balls.. the whole body one long relaxed breath going deeper and deeper and deeper, more relaxed...	D	

Dave Mason © 2009 www.key-hypnosis.com

Sunset Induction

A nice gentle induction linked to memories of the sun going down in a tranquil place.

	SUNSET INDUCTION		
Memory	Imagine you are on an island somewhere... somewhere warm... somewhere nice... imagine you are on that island looking out to sea from some high point... imagine the land beneath you sweeping down towards the sea...	V	
	and it is getting late in the day... and you are relaxing... nothing to do... nothing to do but watch the sun go down... and relax even more...	V	
	and as you are lying there... breathing gently... allow your eyes to close and imagine being on that island... that's right...		
	imagine feeling yourself letting go all the tension of the day... as the sun touches the horizon... and all around things are settling down for the night...	K	
	and that sun will slide down behind the horizon in the time it takes to take ten gentle breaths...	V	bind
	and now breathe out and think to yourself TEN... and imagine that sun going down over a dark red sea...	V	
	and then NINE as you breathe out again that sun slides deeper down ... and things are beginning to get dark...	V	
	and EIGHT... the sun sliding gently down... further down now... and as it sinks deeper you can feel yourself sinking deeper... muscles relaxing... letting go...	K	
	and SEVEN... that sun almost gone now... everything getting dark and quiet and peaceful as the day slips away	K	
	SIX ... going down... imagine the whole world getting darker now... dark and quiet and relaxed and peaceful... and feel yourself releasing, relaxing... letting go and sinking down...	V	
	and FIVE that sun is almost gone... just a soft gentle glow over the dark water...	V	
	and FOUR... all gone... the light fading now... and	K	

	imagine going down into that dark sea... sinking deeper and deeper...		
	And THREE imagine floating weightless in dark blue water... safe and sound... slipping down now... deeper and deeper...	K	
	and TWO floating... drifting...	K	
	and ONE... forgetting about your arms and legs... losing all feeling in your body... allowing your mind to go deeper and deeper...	K	

Dave Mason © 2010 www.key-hypnosis.com

New Year's Eve Induction

The New Years Eve hypnosis script uses the imagery of a clock ticking down to the last seconds to midnight on New Year's Eve, or as we Scots call it, Hogmanay.

This script has a specially written induction and deepener on the New Year theme. You can use it to introduce any kind of therapy based on the idea of a new stage of life, or moving from an old emotional state to a new one.

New Years Eve Induction		
Now imagine yourself in a room somewhere... and it's the 31st of December... coming up to midnight... the last day of the year... soon it will be a new year... maybe a time for a fresh start...	Seeding change	
and take a breath now... and relax as you breathe out... and allow your body to relax completely...		
and focus on your breathing... focus on the gentle in and out of your breath... that's right...		
and now imagine it's the final minute before midnight...		
and in your mind you can begin to count the last ten seconds as the old year runs out... with each breath out count down the numbers... and as you count... each number can allow you to become more relaxed... more comfortable... more at ease...		
TEN...		
NINE... and with each number... times begins to slow... you are relaxing more and more with each breath...		
and EIGHT... all of your body loose and limp and soft and gentle...		
and SEVEN... the breath is making you relax even more now... and you can forget about time... forget about place... nothing matters except breathe and relax...		
SIX... deeper and deeper relaxed... letting go... nothing to do but enjoy that feeling of relaxation...		
FIVE... allow everything to let go... focus on going down and down... more relaxed, more comfortable...		

and FOUR...		
and THREE... more and more comfortable now... your mind can drift away... nothing to do... nothing matters...		
and TWO... more and more loose and relaxed now... arms heavy... legs heavy...		
and ONE... total relaxation...		
New Years Eve Deepener		
and in this relaxed state... you can imagine now... the transition between the Old Year and the New... and imagine ... a scene... a clock tower in a city somewhere... and the hands of the clock reach midnight...		
and as you are lying there... breathing gently... relaxing... imagine that clock striking... and the sound spreading over the city below...		
and as the clock strikes ONE ... the sound of it makes you relax even more...		
and the next strike TWO... as you breath out again... you are sinking down and down...		
and THREE... the third chime takes you even deeper now...		
and FOUR ... and FIVE... each time that clock strikes you feel yourself going deeper and deeper...		
and as you go deeper the sounds of the chimes fades away... all the sounds are fading away now... you are floating... drifting... and your mind can wander away now...		

Dave Mason © 2010 www.key-hypnosis.com

Pace and Lead Inductions

Hand levitation Induction

The Hand Levitation Induction is a simple hypnotic induction. It is said to have been popularised by Milton Erickson.

It is very simple to do, and effective with a wide range of people. It is fun to do at a party or in a bar, particularly with sceptics.

It is basically a pace and lead induction. It works because a suspended hand will naturally tremble, rising and falling slightly. The hypnotist reinforces every upward movement by mentioning it positively, suggesting that the movements will continue, and suggesting that the hand will continue rising: and then links the rising to going into trance... as the hand gets higher the trance gets deeper.

There are several variants of the induction. The hypnotist can choose what to do: just let the hand fall; or suggest it touches the body or face; or even leave it suspended in the air. All these are opportunities for further trance development.

	The Setup		
	Just settle yourself comfortably in that chair... and when you are comfortable... I would like you to lay your arms along the arms of the chair...	I	Seeding comfort, relaxation
	and then choose one arm... and just raise it up slightly so that you hand is hovering about an inch above the chair arm... that's right... raise the whole arm so that your elbow is also about an inch off the chair...		set the arm so that it is floating above the chair arm
	The Induction		
	now just look at your hand... focus on that hand.... notice that the hand is moving very slightly... very slightly upward... that's right it's moving upwards...	I	Dissociation
	and with each movement you feel it getting	D	Pacing

	lighter and lighter... moving up all the time... gently moving... rising...		experience
	that's right... and it's getting lighter and lighter... and maybe now you are becoming aware that your arm is bending at the elbow... as that hand lifts and rises... more and more...	D	Pacing and leading
	[continue pacing and leading, noting and encouraging every movement]		
	it is as if something is lifting that hand... lifting and moving...		Pacing experience
	[the rate of movement usually accelerates after a few small rises, so be careful not to get left behind, start suggesting trance as soon as there is sustained movement. It is also common for the hand to stop half way, just suggest that is exactly as it should be and carry on leading.]		
	and as that hand moves on you may be feeling your eyes are getting heavier... unfocusing... as that hand moves upward... those eyes are getting heavier and heavier...	D	
	and maybe you want to close them now... or when that hand touches your [mention whatever the hand seems be heading for...] chest...	D	Bind of alternatives
	and when that hand touches your chest... your eyes will close completely... and that hand will drop into your lap as quickly as you go into a deep trance... that's right... going into trance now...	D	
	Deepener		
	and with each breath out... you feel yourself going deeper and deeper... more relaxed... more comfortable... more at ease...	>	
	It's as if you have a voice in your head saying... with each breath out... 'Deeper and Deeper'... 'More at ease'... 'Deeper and Deeper'... 'More at ease'...	D	
	And each gentle breath is making you more relaxed... letting go... nothing to do... and just take a few moments to enjoy that wonderful	D	look for eyelid trembling, or

	feeling of relaxation... as every part of your body relaxes deeply... deeply deeply relaxed ... now.	test for eye catalepsy
	[Carry on with the therapy]	

Dave Mason © 2009 www.key-hypnosis.com

Magnetic Hands Induction

The Magnetic Hands Induction is an example of how to turn the client's natural hypnosis ability into a hypnotic induction. The Magnetic Hands induction uses the technique of linking going into trance to some physical movement.

The magnetic hands induction is an old stage hypnosis trick that puts most people into trance very quickly. It can be used to hypnotize a whole audience at once.

It can be used to find the highly hypnotizable people in a group. It works easily and smoothly for most people, but does not work with sceptical people.

If this induction does not work, just tell them it was an experiment and you learned a lot from it. Do not suggest in way that they have failed. Then go on to do another induction such as the staircase induction.

	Magnetic hands induction script		
	Set up		
	The client can be standing or sitting. It will work with a whole room full of people, but this version of the Magnetic Hands induction is for hypnotizing just one person sitting in a chair.		
	I would like you to put your hands out like this. *[Hold your arms up in front of you, straight out at shoulder height as if you are going to take hold of a baby.]*		
	That's right, arms straight out, hands straight out, and with your thumbs pointing up... that's good...		
	Induction		
	Now, I want you to look at that gap between your hands.		
	Keep your eyes focussed on that gap.		Dissociation
	Become aware of the energy in that gap... the energy that exists in that gap between your hands...		Supposition - energy is there
	and now close your eyes and focus on feeling that energy...		Supposition
	and I want you imagine that the energy is like two magnets... as if you have a magnet on the palm of each hand...	V	
	[you can touch the palms of their hands, gently stroking or tapping on their palms, this will cause a		

heightened skin sensation that you can use for suggestion]		
I wonder if you can feel that energy building up?... A powerful magnet on the palm of each hand	I	
and as you focus on that energy... those magnets are getting stronger and stronger... those magnets are getting attracted to each other...	>	
and those magnets are pulling hands in towards each other...	D	
maybe slowly at first.. and them more and more powerfully...		Pace and Lead
you cannot resist that power... those hands are moving closer together		
closer and closer...		Pace and Lead
the attraction is stronger and stronger now... hands moving closer...		
And when those hands touch... you will lose all strength in those arms...		Pace and Lead
and your hands will sink down into lap... and as that happens... every muscle in your body... goes loose and limp and soft ... and you can relax completely now...		
Feel your body relax as that power takes over and lets you relax with confidence... warm and comfortable... totally relaxed...		
That's right... totally relaxed.		
[either do a deepener, or a convincer and then carry on with the therapy]		

Dave Mason © 2009 www.key-hypnosis.com

Hand spread Induction

The Hand Spread Induction is an unusual hypnotic induction.

It is a 'pace and lead induction' and needs good pacing and leading skills. It works because when you spread your hand, your fingers will start to move in on their own unless constant effort is used to keep them apart. The hypnotist paces those movements by suggesting that the movements will continue, that the fingers will continue to move towards each other. As the fingers start moving that movement is linked to suggestions of trance and loss of control... that as the fingers get closer the trance will get deeper.
The hypnotist can aim to get eye closure and then deepen, or can suggest while the fingers are closing that the hand is falling towards the person and when it touches they will go into trance, or that when you snap your fingers, the hand will drop instantly and go into trance.
It is particularly useful when you are hypnotising a client who is standing.

	The Setup		
	Just settle yourself comfortably down... and when you are comfortable... hold your hand up in front of your face, palm towards you, with the fingers spread apart... so you can see the whole hand...	I	Seeding comfort, down
	at a comfortable distance...that's right... just spread those fingers out...		make sure the client is not too long- or short-sighted to see the fingers!
	The Induction		
	now just look at your hand... focus on that hand.... notice that the fingers want to move... moving very slightly... very slightly moving together... that's right moving together...	I	Dissociation
	and with each movement of one finger... other fingers start to move as well... small jerky	D	Pacing experience

	movements perhaps... moving... relaxing...	D	
	that's right... and those fingers are moving closer and closer... and I wonder if you have noticed yet that your arm is bending at the elbow... as those fingers get closer and closer... more and more...	D	Pacing and leading
	[continue pacing and leading, noting and gently encouraging every movement]		
	it is as if something is pulling that hand... pulling it towards you... as those fingers get closer and closer...	I	Pacing experience
	[the movement of the fingers is usually jerky and uneven, so keep encouraging in a soft voice, start suggesting trance as soon as there is sustained movement. It is also common for the hand and arm to waver up and down, just suggest that is exactly as it should be and carry on leading.]		
	and as that hand moves towards you and those fingers are closing and you are hearing my voice you may be feeling your eyes are getting heavier... unfocusing... as that hand falls towards you... those eyes are getting heavier and heavier...	D	
	and maybe it would be more comfortable to close them now... or when that hand touches your [mention whatever the hand seems be heading for...] face... and those fingers are almost completely relaxed now...	D	Bind of alternatives
	and when that hand touches... or gets close enough... your eyes will close completely... and that hand will drop into your lap as quickly as you go into a deep trance... that's right... going into trance now...	D	
	Deepener		
	and with each breath out... allow yourself to go deeper and deeper... more relaxed... more comfortable... more at ease...	>	
	It's as if you have a voice in your head saying... with each breath out... 'Deeper and Deeper'... 'More at ease'... 'Deeper and Deeper'... 'More at	D	pace with the out breath, very

	ease'...	slowly
	And each gentle breath is making you more relaxed... letting go... nothing to do... and just take a few moments to enjoy that wonderful feeling of relaxation... as every part of your body relaxes deeply... deeply deeply relaxed ... now.	D look for eyelid trembling, or change in breathing pattern
	[Now do a convincer]	eye catalepsy, or finger lift etc.
	[Carry on with the therapy]	

Dave Mason © 2009 www.key-hypnosis.com

Two Word Induction

Description: The Two Word Induction is the simplest induction around.

Procedure: All you have to do is watch the client breathe, and say two words on each breath out. The repetition and breathing calms the nervous client, and its gentle take-your-time approach lulls away anxiety about being able to go into trance.

Advantages: This induction is very hard to get wrong - gentle breathing automatically induces trance. The client can take as long as they want. It teaches you to watch the client for signs of trance.

Uses: For clients who are too nervous for other inductions.

Extensions: Once you understand the principle you will be able to do this type of inductions with any key words.

	The Setup		
	Just settle down now... get yourself comfortable in the chair...		
	Have you got any worries about going into trance?		
	[Deal with whatever the client says]		
	I am glad you have brought that up... that helps me a lot... many people are afraid to say what they think, aren't they?...		Reassure they are doing it right
	Is your head comfortable there?.. just move your arms and legs around to get really comfortable... ready to go into trance... that's right...	I	Break any rigid posture...
	Now, all I am going to do is to ask you to breathe...		
	I want you to become aware of your breathing... nothing else... just think about your breathing... that's all you have to do...		Reassurance
	Now, take a breath and just let it go... that's good...		PACE BREATHING
	Take another breath and let it go... that's OK, isn't it?		Reassurance
	Now think about your breath... as you breathe in...		
	as you breathe in... notice how far down your throat you can actually feel the air going down... you can notice the air	I	Dissociation - focus on body

	passing the back of your nose... going down... and then deeper...		sensations
	and with the next breath ... notice how aware you can become of what you feel inside your body...		
The Induction			
BREATHING IN	[Watch the client breathing. With each breath say...] That's Right.	I	
	That's right.	I	
	That's right.	I	
	[Now start pacing their breathing... say That's right with every breath... but once you have the rhythm, start slowing your words, so the client slows their breathing... to match the speed at which you are saying That's right.]	>	
	[When they are breathing gently and regularly switch the focus to the out breath]		
BREATHING OUT	Now focus on each gentle breath as it flows out... imagine that with every breath you are saying to yourself... Deeper and Deeper... More and More relaxed...	D	PACE BREATHING
	[next breath]... with every breath out you are saying to yourself... Deeper and Deeper... More and More relaxed...	D	
	[next breath]... allow yourself to feel more and more relaxed...	D	
	[next breath]... That's right...	I	
	[Continue pacing their breathing... say That's right with every breath out... start slowing your words even more, so the client slows their breathing... until the client is breathing softly from the top of their chest... If they cough or move or show signs they have not relaxed enough, go back to an earlier stage and keep pacing their breathing.]		
	That's right.	I	
SIGNS OF TRANCE	[You should see signs of trance... eyelids fluttering... face relaxed... head jerking		

	slightly... long slow breathing... head falling forward... body immobile and slumped.]		
	That's right...	I	
	[Do a depth test or use a deepener, then carry on with the session]		

Christmas Tree Induction

This induction focuses on a Christmas tree and uses all the associations people have with Christmas to transfer feelings to the tree.
It uses the idea of lights getting darker linked to breathing and then links darker to more relaxed and induces trance by pacing the breathing.

	CHRISTMAS TREE INDUCTION		
Memory	I wonder if you can remember a time ... a long time ago... round about Christmas time... when you were much younger...		dissociation
Memory	allow your mind to go back... think about a past Christmas... a time when the feeling was laid-back and cruising... a time to relax and feel good...		reconnection
	and maybe you can remember a quiet room... and time on your own... a quiet place somewhere... to just enjoy the season...	V	away from the here and now
	and maybe you can close your eyes as you are relaxing now and think about that feeling...		eye closure
	think about that feeling of calm and peace...	K	
	and a room somewhere... with decorations... lights... Christmas tinsel... all the things you associate with that time of the year...and a tree... a tree with lights... and decorations... and in your mind you see that tree, all lit up with soft lights... in a room that's dark and dim... and there is just the lights of the tree... and dark all around...	V	set the scene
	and as you think about that tree... remembering Christmases past... relaxing, breathing quietly... become aware of the gentle rise and fall of your breath... and focus on that breathing... breathing in... breathing out... that's right...		pace and lead
	and as you think about your breathing... and those memories of Christmas... you notice with each breath out... those lights appear a little more dim... and as you breath out again... the lights on the tree become darker still... and you become aware that with each breath you are becoming more relaxed... and you can begin to enjoy a	D	Metaphor dim = deepening trance

	pleasant feeling of control... and you can begin to wonder about those lights...		
	and on the next breath, imagine the lights at the top of the tree becoming dim and dark...		
	and then another relaxing breath and the lights further down the tree are also growing dim and dark...		
	and another breath... and more of that tree is going dark now... and all around in that room, everything is becoming quiet and peaceful...		
	and as you continue there... breathing quietly... thinking of those lights... and that feeling of peace and contentment... allow that feeling to spread...		
	and as that feeling spreads... become aware of a heaviness in your arms and legs... a heaviness in your muscle and hands... your eyes... and imagine that feeling spreading... relaxing all the muscles of your face... and letting go... and your shoulders are tired and heavy...	I	physical relaxation
	and as you feel that spreading... that Christmas tree... is becoming darker and softer... and more blurred... and all the lights have faded away to nothing...		
	and in that room... peaceful and quiet... a soft gentle darkness... and as you relax more... everything is slipping away... and in that dark place there is just the hint of dim colors... reflecting from wrappings and ornaments...		
	and all the colors begin to swirl around... and you feel yourself floating... drifting... swirling... as they carry you down... deeper and deeper... relaxing... breathing gently... letting it all go now...		Trance

Dave Mason © 2010 www.key-hypnosis.com

Pendulum Hypnosis Induction Script

This is a fun script that you can use for a bit of guerrilla hypnosis. It is really a trick, but you can use it convince people that you have magic powers, or you can tell them that it is all being caused by the power of hypnosis.

In fact, the pendulum moves because of tiny tremors in the muscles of the hand of the person holding the pendulum. It cannot not move. All you have to do is to suggest that you are causing the movement, and the person will believe you, because it really is moving and they don't know why.

Gullible people have been taken in by this demonstration for centuries, and it is still used by fortune tellers today. I have added an induction on to the end. It works well at parties to demonstrate your skill.

	The Set up		
Set up	[The person should be sitting down. It can be at table or just in a seat of some sort.]		
	You will need a pendulum. This can be any sort of small weight on a bit of string, it really doesn't matter. If you are going to do it regularly put a piece of crystal on the end of a fine silver chain. The pendulum string needs to be about half the length of the forearm if at a table, or about the length of the lower leg to use it on the floor. Do not allow the person to support their wrist with the other arm.		
	Pendulum Susceptibility Test		
	Are you ready to test the power of hypnosis?	Yes Set 1	
	Are you ready to find out at what your own mind can do?	Yes Set 2	
	Are you willing to learn something you never expected?	Yes Set 3	
	Take this pendulum and hold between your thumb and index finger and let it hang over the table [(or over the floor)]. Just let it hang straight down. Make sure your elbow is supported and your hand is vertically above the pendulum.		

	Move your hand up or down until the weight at the end is almost touching the surface.		Get them to loosen up the arm
	Now touch the pendulum on the surface and then lift it slightly. The pendulum should be at a complete stop; just hanging down.		Start from steady
	Now, focus your attention on the pendulum. Really concentrate on the weight at the end of the pendulum... keep your eyes on that weight...		Focus of attention
	Now as you focus you will find the end of that pendulum will begin to swing...	D	Direct suggestion
	And the more you focus... the more that pendulum wants to swing...	>	Multiplier
	now just imagine that pendulum beginning to swing... and the pendulum is starting to follow your thoughts... as you visualize it... that pendulum is swinging more and more... responding to your thoughts...	D	More suggestion
	Watch as that pendulum begins to sway and swing... sway and swing... back and forth... back and forth... that's right...	D	First test
	Just let it happen...	I	will happen
	swinging more and more now...	D	confirm
	and now imagine that pendulum slowing down... slowing down now... [Pace with the movement and their breathing]...	D	
	that pendulum is slowing down... coming to a complete stop...	D	
	[Doesn't matter if it stops or not... keep on with the suggestions]		
	and now imagine that pendulum beginning to swing the other way... side to side... or in circles...	I	Second test
	and you may be surprised at what it does...	D	Bind
Pendulum Induction			
	[the pendulum will be either swinging side to side or round in circles. Use whatever it is doing and link it to suggestions of going into trance. This assumes a circular movement is going on.]		
	and as that circle goes round... round and round,,, follow it with your eyes...	D	

Behavior	and as that circle is going round... those eyes are getting heavier... getting tired... and as the circle continues to go round... your eyes are blinking more... getting more tired... tired and heavy ... and the pendulum is getting heavy... getting so heavy ... it is slowing down...	D	
	and as it slows down... your eyes are going down... the pendulum is heavy... your eyes are heavy ... your eyes are closing... your fingers are opening...	D	
	the pendulum is getting too heavy to hold ... as your eyes are getting too heavy... closing down... that pendulum is getting heavy too... and you are losing control of those fingers... and fingers are opening... eyes closing... relaxing... letting everything go...	D	
	Termination		
	[when the pendulum drops the person has gone into trance].		

Dave Mason © 2011 www.key-hypnosis.com

Relaxation Inductions

Relaxation Induction

The Visualisation Induction is a gentle hypnotic induction based on the mind's ability to imagine a state of relaxation. Imagining the relaxation causes your muscles to remember times like that, and as the listener remembers the physical changes it becomes easier to pace and lead them into some gentle fantasy.

It works because when you visualise something, you must 'go inside', so you dissociate yourself from the present. It happens naturally while watching movies and or playing computer games. It is sometimes called 'being in the zone'.

By giving the listener a pleasant visualisation you get them to go into 'trance' by themselves. It is quite easy to do as long as you are careful to keep the listener in the 'state'. If you say anything harsh, or if you use images that clash, you will jolt them right out of trance. But once you understand the principle you will be able to do stealth inductions based on anything.

This is a lovely exercise to do with someone you are close to, in an intimate setting such as sitting together quietly.

Just start talking softly with '*I wonder if you can imagine lying somewhere on a summer afternoon...*' and in a minute or two your partner will have drifted off into trance... and you can then build that into any kind of visualisation you want to. Especially useful as a way to start a playful erotic interlude.

	The Visualisation		
memory	I wonder if you can think back to an earlier time... a time when you lay down somewhere on a hot sunny day... and maybe it was in a park or a garden ... or it could have been on a roof or somewhere... on a bright day...		seed some relaxing scene
memory	and how when you look at the sun with your eyes closed... somehow you can still see that bright light through your eyelids... and as you lie there remembering that light... and breathing gently... and remembering what it is like to lie in a comfortable place somewhere... and feel the support under your back and under your legs...		evoke a memory of relaxation

	and on a warm day you can feel so drowsy... so ready to drift away... and maybe you can imagine lying in a park somewhere... or a garden... or a beach... and I wonder what you would hear... maybe you could hear children playing... people talking... and the way that their voices can just fade away... like a radio being turned right down...	I	suggestions of drifting... turning things down...
	as you lie there... peacefully relaxed...just feeling yourself supported... and your own weight pressing down...	K	pace and lead on muscle relaxation
	and maybe there is a gentle breeze... that just riffles your hair... and a warm sun caressing your face... and your arms... and as you lie there every muscle can become... limp and loose...	K	use all sensations, touch, warmth,
memory	It's so good to just totally relax... just let everything go... and you might remember... when you could just relax and enjoy that peace and calm... and just think how good it is... to enjoy relaxing... nothing to do... nothing to worry about...		recall a pleasant time
	[either do a deepener, or carry on gently suggesting visualisations involving peace, calm, relaxation]	I	

Dave Mason © 2009 www.key-hypnosis.com

Fisherman's Induction

The Fisherman's Induction is an example of how to use the person's interest or hobby as the basis of hypnosis induction.

Procedure: Any hobby has the ability to pull the person into 'the zone' where they lose track of time and are fully focused on the activity. You can remind them of that experience, and as the listener remembers how it was they are actually dissociating, and while they are in that state you lead them gently into trance.

Method: It works because when you remember the experience of something, you must 'go inside', so you dissociate yourself from the present. It happens naturally which is why we enjoy hobbies. It is quite easy to do as long as you are careful to keep the listener in the 'state'. If you say anything harsh, or if you use images that clash, you will jolt them right out of trance.

Advantages: once you understand the principle you will be able to do inductions based on any absorbing hobby or interest.

	Drifting off while fishing		
	I wonder if you can think back to a warm day... a time when you were fishing... and take a few moments to think about how relaxing fishing can be... what you enjoy about fishing... getting away from everything... the calm tranquil moments... [pause]		seed remembrance of a familiar experience
memory	and bring to mind that feeling of being totally absorbed in fishing... not really thinking of anything... your body relaxed and easy... the line going into the water... nothing to worry about... just enjoying the time passing pleasantly...		dissociation
memory	and as you lie there now... breathing softly... remembering that experience.. ... remembering what it is like to be fishing comfortably somewhere... like you feel the chair supporting you... comfortably... relaxing...		evoke a memory of relaxation
	and on a warm day you can feel so drowsy... so ready to drift away... and imagine being in a boat somewhere... fishing... drifting... and the warm day can make you feel like closing your eyes to remember that feeling better...	V	suggestions of drifting...

	as you lie there... peacefully relaxed... and your arms and legs heavy and limp... head relaxing... eyes closed... each breath relaxing you more...	I	pace and lead on muscle relaxation
	and imagine being on that boat... the warm day... the boat gently rocking... waves lightly rippling along the hull.... soft light reflecting off the ripples on the water... the gentle motion of the boat... gently moving up and down... and down and down....	V	use all sensations, touch, warmth,
	and the line going down... down into the water... and imagine that in your mind you can follow that line down into the water... imagine sliding down that line... sliding imperceptibly deeper... and in the water... warm... floating... peaceful... calm... and a soft greenish light all around... and in that clear water you feel safe and relaxed... you can see the bright water all around you... and the line going deeper down... and as you follow that line down the water changes... gets a little darker... going a soft blue colour... and you feel more comfortable... gently, slowly drifting down... as you look down... into the depths...the water becomes a deep dark blue colour... and you feel yourself letting go... trusting the water to keep you safe as you slowly and comfortably drift down deeper and deeper....	V	
memory	and far below... vague shapes... slowly moving... circling... drawing you ever deeper... and relaxing...		images of depth and tranquillity
	[either do a deepener, or carry on gently suggesting visualisations involving peace, calm, relaxation and then do the therapy]		
		I	

Dave Mason © 2009 www.key-hypnosis.com

Deep Blue Induction

This induction is a nice way put people into trance by using a gentle relaxation. It is in the same class of inductions as the Fisherman's Induction, but in this case the person can imagine what it would be like to relax on a boat even if they have never been on one. The actual induction mechanism is the idea of sliding done a line, not the relaxation.

Procedure: It works by asking the client to 'let go' without saying how they should do so. It is based on a continually developing metaphor of things getting darker and quieter as you go deeper.

Method: The Deep Blue Induction works by comparing something people know how to do, letting go physically, with something they think they might not be able to do, letting go mentally.

Advantages: It is useful when the client says they are afraid they won't know what to do to go into trance.

Disadvantages: Not for people who have difficulty visualising and check they are not afraid of water.

Uses: It is a nice alternative to the standard induction and works with most people. It can also be used as a deepener.

TARGET	INDUCTION TEXT	COMMENTS
Memory	I wonder if you can remember a time you were on a boat... and it was a nice day... and you were able to relax and enjoy some time off...	Dissociation
	or maybe you can imagine an ideal getaway on a private boat... anchoring in some remote location...	Visualisation
	Now just imagine that you are out on that boat... out on the water somewhere on a lazy day... and imagine you are lying in a really comfortable chair or something like that on that boat... and around you you have everything you could want... and there is nobody to bother you... just you and the quiet water and the freedom to stretch out all the way... and it's a lovely day and the sun is shining... big blue sky...	Dissociation Allow the listener to have what they need to relax
	water gently rippling underneath the hull... a sound that reminds you that you can cast off and drift away on the current if you want to ...	Utilise sounds
Memory	and the boat on the water... rocking gently... first one side... and then the other... and gradually	Utilise motion

	you can feel yourself relaxing in that chair thinking about the motion... just remembering what it is like to be rocked gently... softly... side to side ... relaxing	
	and feel your arms getting loose and limp... and you legs are relaxing... letting go ... loose and relaxed...	suggest muscular relaxation
	and on that boat it is the sort of day where you don't wan't to do anything... The kind of day you say to yourself 'just lie down and let your mind drift'...	
	and just enjoy being out there... away from everything... no phones... no worries... enjoying being out there... away from it all... leaving everything behind...	
	Then imagine a fishing line... imagine the fishing line going into the water... and what it would be like to follow that fishing line down... in your mind...	
	and you could go down the first couple of metres... feel safe and warm... surrounded by lovely clear bright water... imagine what it wouild be like to be a fish just hanging there... motionless... breathing easily...	
	and then you can just let go... allow yourself to drift down a few more feet... deeper and deeper... down and down... and the waters around you begin to change colour... gets a little darker...	
	And then again... you let go a little... let out the tension... and you feel yourself going down a few more feet... and you are just lying there.. suspended... weightless... cool and calm...	
	and you let go a little more... and you sink gently down a little more...	
	and everything round about is becoming a lovely calming soothing deep blue colour...	
	And far above is the boat and the line leading down... and you are feeling detached... drifting... easy... floating...	
	And you realise you are letting go more and	

	more... drifting deeper and deeper down and down... that lovely warm safe feeling... down and down	
	And you let go some more... and slip soundlessly down into the twilight depths... quiet and calm and peaceful...	
Memory	and you find yourself suspended... motionless... breathing easily... like being held, cradled... like holding a baby in your arms... breathing gently... not a care in the world... trusting drifting off to sleep... comfortable... secure...	Link to memories of sleeping
	And far away to each side... clear dark water... everything is calm and peaceful... far below the chattering waves... you allow your mind to float free...	
	Release... let go... down and down into the deep dark blue water... and all round you... endless space ... floating ... totally relaxed... completely at ease...	
	and allow your mind to drift out into that deep ocean beyond thought... search and explore the ocean of the mind... red and gold and green... all the colours of the deep mind...	
	opening and rolling away like wave... and in that place you become aware of shapes... things moving... changing... flashes of light... shadows and moonbeams... glimpses of hands...eyes... faces... flickering fireflies in the forest of thoughts..	
	and once again you let go... just releasing everything... open to whatever comes... waiting in a place without time or space... drifting deeper and deeper	

David Mason   www.key-hypnosis.com © 2010

The self induction induction

Method: The laziest way to put someone in trance is by getting them to hypnotise themselves. You give the listener their instructions and then just wait for them to signal that they are ready. It couldn't be simpler.

Uses: The Self Induction Induction appears to be little used but actually works very well.

Advantages: It is particularly useful for clients who will not go into trance with normal methods because they are afraid of losing control.

Extensions: It is also extremely effective and fast for people who have some experience of meditation or martial arts mind techniques.

	Self induced trance	
	OK. I want you to understand that you are in control... you are in control at all times... and you can decide exactly how and when you go into trance...	Bind
	Just settle back and make yourself comfortable.... Let your arms flop and let your hands relax... maybe shrug your shoulders a little... let your head recline and settle down... jiggle your legs if you want... until things are just the way you want them...	Bodily relaxation
	And now you can take a deep breath... hold that breath ... and as you let it go... allow that breath out to close your eyes...	Eyes closed
	That's good.	Reassurance
	And now take another breath... and hold it... and this time as you breath out... really relax... just become aware of any tension in your muscles... and allow it to relax...	Progressive relaxation
Memory	And when you are ready... take another breath and hold it... and just think about how relaxed you can be... I wonder when was the time you were most relaxed?... I wonder how relaxed it's possible to be?...	Transderivational Search
	And you can now let your breathing go back to normal... just focus on your	Pace with breathing

	breathing... focus on that gentle movement of air... in ... and out.... in... and out.....	
Capability	That's very good... you're doing very well...	Reassurance
	and just think about each breath out... feeling more and more relaxed... more at ease... more comfortable... That's right...	
	and with each breath out... you can imagine your own voice in your head... or someone speaking... saying "deeper and deeper"... "more and more"... relaxing...	Using their own 'voice' to deliver the instructions.
	and you can choose how much you want to let go with every breath... and part of your mind can go into trance and while part of your mind can stay alert... and while that part is as alert as you want it to be it can be deciding how deeply you want that other part to go... and let that other part go...	Bind
	and all the while... breathing gently... choosing how deeply to go... continue breathing... relaxing... watching as part of your mind is going deeper... as your inner voice leads you... down and down...	Supposition
	until when you are at right depth for you... allow your mind to choose... one hand or other... and you can be curious as how your mind chooses... one hand instead of the other... as if it is someone else's hand...	Dissociation
	and you'll know when your mind has chosen... you can allow a finger or a thumb or maybe something else to signal that you have reached a comfortable depth... and allow that finger or thumb to move on its own... just let it happen... when it's ready...	Dissociation
	[await signal]	

\

Dave Mason © 2009 www.key-hypnosis.com

Walk in the Park Induction

A visualization and breathing induction based on memories of a slow gentle walk outdoors. Using memories this way allows the mind to slip into trance almost without noticing.

	Walk in the park Induction Script		
	I once had an old friend who liked to go for walks... walks around town... walks in the country... walks by the shore...and no matter where you are... my friend said... you can always find a pleasant walk ...	I	Dissociation
Memory	And I wonder if you can remember a time...when you went for a walk ... somewhere nice... just for relaxation... maybe by a river... or in the country... or it could be a park or somewhere like that		Invoke memories of relaxation
Memory	and maybe if you closed your eyes you can remember how pleasant it is... enjoying that feeling you get ...when you are amongst trees and grass and things you like... and far away from things that might disturb you...	I	Time congruency
Memory	... people remember different things... the breeze in your hair... the swish of your clothes as you walk ... the warm sun on your face... maybe the feel of soft earth under your feet... the smell of new cut grass or country air... sounds of the outdoors... freedom... times like that can make you feel so good...		using all the modalities Truism
	and maybe if you take a deep breath now you can feel that feeling... that relaxation... now... as you breathe out...		Breathing = relaxing
	and with each gentle breath out you might like to wonder how relaxed you can become... and you might be feeling that relaxation starting... and spreading...		Breathing induction
	and sometimes in times like that you find your mind drifting away...	I	Dissociation

to some place away from here... and you find yourself on a gravel path... and you can feel the gravel crunching under your feet... you can hear each step... as you go along comfortably... wondering where this path might take you... and all around there's sunshine... trees... flowers... everything is calm ... and there's a sense of quiet and expectancy...	Seeding 'comfortable'	
and the path goes along and down into a dell... you have to go down a number of steps... and each step takes you down... deeper and deeper... you go down each step... and counting... Five... deeper and deeper... Four... deeper and more relaxed... three... deeper and deeper... Two... so relaxed... One... maybe more relaxed than you have ever been in your whole life...	Countdown deepener	
[either do a deepener, or a convincer and then carry on with the therapy]		

David Mason   www.key-hypnosis.com © 2011

Analytical Client Induction

Technique: The Analytical Induction was developed by David Mason of Key Hypnosis as a way of hypnotizing clients who would not or could not relax enough for normal induction methods. It is a very gentle induction method that uses the body's natural parasympathetic system to put the client into trance without anxiety or fears of losing control. You use the affirmation wording to put whatever idea you want to into the client's mind, while at the same time inducing trance.

Advantages: It works well even for analytical people who normally are hard to hypnotize. It prevents their over active minds and constant self talk from interfering with the induction process. It also has the advantage that the actual words can be varied to suit each individual.

Disadvantages: The hypnotist needs to be able to recognise when trance has been achieved as there is little feedback from the client.

Extensions: The affirmation breathing induction is better and more efficient than the mantra inductions used for meditation. It is very effective for hypnotizing yourself. It is a very good way of teaching self hypnosis to clients.

You can make up any pair of affirmations: for weight loss, or smoking or anything you like as long as they are brief and easy to say.

The Setup		
Just make yourself comfortable now... settle into a position where you can begin to relax...	I	Seeding comfort, relaxation
Now take one deep breath... and release...		Parasympathetic
And another deep breath... and release again... just let it all go...		response
and one last breath... and this time really relax as you breath out...		begins
That's right...		Reassurance
The Induction	I	
Now allow your breathing to return to normal...		
and focus on your breathing... just become aware of the gentle in and out of your breath...		Dissociation
That's right...		
Think about how your breath comes in and goes out... and imagine that as you breath out ... each breath can relax you a little more...	D	Suggest Relaxation
and with each breath in... say to yourself... quietly in your mind... *'I want this to work'*....		Start the affirmation

and with each breath out... say to yourself... quietly in your mind... *'It's working now'...*	Second affirmation
and with each breath in... *'I want this to work'*	Pace the breathing
and with each breath out... say to yourself... *'It's working now...'*	Pace the breathing
[Watch the client breathing... with each breath in speak aloud the in breath affirmation softly and quietly... then the out breath affirmation... keep repeating the affirmations to remind the client until they start showing signs of going into trance...]	Take as long as necessary, just watch the client
[Pace the client's breathing... and lead them into slower and slower breaths... after a dozen breaths or so you should see signs of trance, eyelids flickering, swallowing, head jerking... etc...]	Start leading
[As soon as the client shows signs of going into trance stop repeating the affirmation and let them carry on...]	
And with each breath out... you are going deeper and deeper... more and more relaxed...	
deep... deeply, deeply relax...	
That's right...	
[It is a good idea to do a finger lift to test for depth of trance]	
[Carry on with the therapy]	

Breathing Affirmation Pairs... select a pair that match the issues of the particular client
I want this to work... it's working now
Do it often... do it right
Whatever it takes... Ready to go
Nothing important... letting it go
Fears examined... melt away
Go... with the flow
I am ready now... show me the way

Open to love... love is all
Bless me... and keep me
Seeking and finding... beauty within
Whatever comes... I can do it
A drop of water... wears down stone
Breathing gently... calmly down
Constant helper... faithful friend
Steady progress... happy end
Not my problem... fades away
Still and silence... peace and calm
Life is for living... sweeten the days
love and laughter... living well
Sunny mornings... happy days
Softly gently... turning it round
Power and beauty... only the best
Deep inside... things unfolding
Paths before me... show the way
Silently connecting... the universe within
Positive way ... to positive change

Now add your own ...

David Mason   www.key-hypnosis.com © 2010

Instant and Rapid Inductions

The Instant Induction is used by stage hypnotists and entertainer to produce a sudden and dramatic hypnotic trance aimed at impressing people.

Method: The way it works is quite simple. There is very little dialog, although there is often quite a prolonged build up to it. The client is usually taken by the hand and the hypnotist starts talking to the client or distracting him in some way. The moment the client is distracted, the hypnotist suddenly jerks the client's arm, pulling him off balance and shouts 'sleep'. The suddenness causes the client to become disoriented, and the hypnotist immediately begins to give the client suggestions about relaxing, staying calm, letting go, going deeper... and so on. The instructions must be given the instant the client gets jerked off balance. If the suggestions are not given within the first few seconds of the disorientation, the client will begin to reorient himself and will pop out of trance as fast as he went in.

The reason it works is due to the startle reflex. Most animals have an instinct to 'freeze' at sudden danger. This is a very primitive response and in humans what it does is to instantly turn off the conscious mind and pass control to the unconscious mind. In the few seconds while the unconscious mind is busy assessing the nature of the threat, there is an opportunity to put suggestions directly into the unconscious mind, and have the unconscious mind act on them.

Uses: This induction is most often seen at religious revivalist type meetings. The evangelist whips up the crowd and builds excitement and expectation with music, lights and repetition. Selected people are then invited on to the stage. Most of them will already be in a light hypnotic state due to the emotional intensity they are feeling. The evangelist will then take their right hand in his left hand and distract the person by passing his right hand in front of their face and raising it high and shouting something out loud. As the words are shouted the evangelist pulls hard on the person's right hand unexpectedly pulling them off balance. This creates the startle response and the person collapses into the arm of waiting attendants.

Disadvantages: Instant inductions are seldom used by therapeutic hypnotists because the client often feels frightened, or bewildered at what is going on, and some people spontaneously snap right out of it again.

Extensions: Once you understand the principle you will be able to do instant inductions based on any kind of sudden movement.

Instant Induction - Standing

	The Setup		
	Arrange it so that the client is standing directly in front of you, at a comfortable distance.		
	Take the client's right hand in your right hand. It doesn't matter if the client is right or left handed.	D	
	The CLASSIC STANDING INSTANT Induction		
	Move the hand around a little, as if you are testing to know how relaxed the client's arm is. This is just a distraction. It has no purpose.	I	
	As you move the hand around ask "Are you feeling relaxed now?"	D	
	The client will say 'Yes' or 'No'. Whatever the answer say 'Yes, I can feel that'.		
	Then ask the client a distracting question, all the while gently moving the hand a little. For example, 'Is you wife in the audience? Did you find your seats all right?'		
	You will see the client's eyes defocus as he thinks about the question, possibly his eyes will move up and to his left as he tries to visualise the response.		
	The moment you see that his focus has gone inwards, a) with your right hand, pull hard and down on his right hand so that his arm comes towards you		
	and at the same time,		
	b) step forward and put your weight on your left foot,		
	and at the same time,		
	c) shout loudly directly in his ear 'SLEEP!'		
	and at the same time,		
	d) with your left hand, reach up and pull his right shoulder forward		
	e) keep pulling with both hands until he starts to fall off balance		

as he is falling off balance towards you		
f) transfer all your weight on to your left leg and prepare to take the client's weight as he falls against you.		
The client will be momentarily losing the power in his legs as his mind goes into the startle reflex		
YOU MUST TAKE CONTROL AT THIS POINT. YOU MUST START SPEAKING IMMEDIATELY.		
g) Take the client's weight so that he does not actually fall		
h) Say firmly and confidently in quiet voice, directly into his ear (his head will be right up against you at this point) 'You are safe. Your legs will hold you up. Allow your mind to go deeply into relaxation. Just relax your body now. Allow your head to fall forward, really relaxed. All of your muscles are going loose and limp and your mind is relaxing and going deeper. And your arms are hanging loose and heavy... your head is loose and heavy...You can enjoy this feeling of total relaxation as your mind drifts away. Everything is safe and controlled for you now... Just relax.... that's right'.		
'And now just allow that feeling to continue... going deeper and more relaxed... nothing to think about... mind just drifting away... as you stand there totally relaxed... '		
[And then continue with whatever you want to demonstrate.]		

Dave Mason © 2009 www.key-hypnosis.com

Instant inductions can be done to anyone, anywhere, but you need to take care when doing instant induction hypnosis. Rapid inductions can be fun, but make sure when you are hypnotizing someone that they have consented to be hypnotized. Otherwise the outcome of the instant induction might be an instantly angry person. Instant hypnosis can be distressing if it is unexpected hypnosis. Rapid inductions are very powerful, be sure that you are ready to handle the result.

Instant Induction – Sitting

	The Setup		
	To start the instant induction arrange it so that the client is sitting in front of you, at a comfortable distance. Position yourself so that you are to the right of the client. It doesn't matter if you are sitting or standing.		
	It doesn't matter if the client is right or left handed.		
	The Classic Sitting Instant Induction		
	Tell the client to extend their right arm with the palm facing down. Their arm doesn't have to be straight.		
	Push the back of their hand down with your left hand, just gently, and let them resist you. This is just so can get your left hand near them in a natural sort of way Ask them if they can feel the resistance.		
	The client will say 'Yes' or 'No'. Whatever the answer say 'Yes, I can feel that'.		
	Then ask the client a distracting question, all the while gently pressing down and letting the client move their hand up again. For example, 'Are you quite comfortable with that? '		
	Then smoothly move your right hand under the palm of their right hand with your hand facing upwards, and take your left hand away and put it on their shoulder.		
	Tell the client ' Now, start pressing down on my hand'.		
	as they press down, increase the strength of your upward force to match it, so their hand stays where it is and doesn't drop.		
	Say to client 'Keep pressing down, that's right'.		
	The client will press some more... keep resisting so that there is quite an upward pressure to keep it from dropping down...		
	Say to the client, in an exasperated tone...' I said press down...'.		
	The client is actually pressing down quite hard, so usually they will look at you...		
	You will see the client's eyes defocus as he thinks about what you just said, maybe shows a little		

annoyance... At that point the client has forgotten all about the hand and is wondering what to do or say next... .		
The moment you see that the focus has gone inwards, a) pull your right hand away suddenly, so that his hand goes down		
and at the same time,		
b) use your left hand behind the client's right shoulder and pull forward sharply,		Be careful not to do it too hard
and at the same time,		
c) shout loudly 'SLEEP!' (it actually doesn't matter what you shout, but SLEEP is traditional).		
The client will momentarily lose the power to respond as his mind goes into the startle reflex		
YOU MUST TAKE CONTROL AT THIS POINT. YOU MUST START SPEAKING IMMEDIATELY.		
d) Put your right hand on the client's head and gently (gently!) push the client into a more upright position, and start to gently rotate their head just a little. This adds further to the disorientation.		Safety!
and at the same time,		
e) *Say firmly and confidently in a quiet voice,* 'You are safe. You can relax now. Allow your mind to go deeply into relaxation. Just relax your body now. Allow your body to relax completely, really relaxed. All of your muscles are going loose and limp and your mind is relaxing and going deeper. And your arms are hanging loose and heavy... your head is loose and heavy...You can enjoy this feeling of total relaxation as your mind drifts away. Everything is safe and controlled for you now... Just relax.... that's right'.		
'And now just allow that feeling to continue... going deeper and more relaxed... nothing to think about... mind just drifting away... as you sit there totally relaxed... '		
[And then continue with whatever you want to demonstrate.]		

	Safety Note: Make sure the client cannot fall out of the chair, be ready to take the weight and gently put them back in the chair. Do not be alarmed if the clients eyes are partly open and they roll their eyes up so that just the whites are showing. It is just a normal response to the startle reflex. When you are learning instant inductions use the minimum amount of force, do not jerk people around, you can injure their muscles. It only needs a gentle push on the shoulder. Be very careful when moving their head, the movement is soft, slow and minimal: if there is any doubt, don't.		

Dave Mason © 2009 www.key-hypnosis.com

Stage hypnotist Rapid Induction

Procedure: One of the simplest rapid inductions. Use this to hypnotise groups of people on stage very quickly. This way the audience will not lose interest while waiting for each person to be induced separately.

Method: It works by
  (1) inducing muscular tension and expectation,
  (2) progressively releasing that tension at the same time controlling the client's breathing,
  (3) inducing dissociation through visualisation and cleverly incorporating 'down', 'dark' and 'calm' in one mental image.

Advantages: Fast, reliable. Trance can usually be achieved in less than two minutes with any number of people at the same time. It also works very well in a clinical situation.

Disadvantages: Some people do not respond to the visualisation.

Uses: Good for a group induction.

Good way to teach clients self hypnosis. Show them how it works by putting them into trance first, and then get them to go through the stages while you supervise, and after that they will be able to go into trance whenever they want to.

1.		*Put the body into a rigid, uncomfortable position*	
		Now, sit back in the chair,	
	Toes	Raise your toes off the ground,	
	Hands	Place your hands on your knees, arms outstretched, palms facing up.	
	Head	Tilt your head back as far as it will go	
	Eyes	Roll your eyes up so that you are looking at a point on the ceiling behind the chair.	
2.		*Begin the physical relaxation*	
	Eyes	Now take a nice deep breath... and as you breathe out, let your eyes close...	
	Head	Now breathe in,... and as you breathe out, let your head fall into a comfortable position...	
	Hands	Now breathe in... and as you breathe out... let your hands and arms relax...	
	Shoulders	Now breathe in... and as you breathe out, make your shoulders sag down	

	Feet	Now breathe in ... and as you breathe out, let your feet go to rest flat on the floor	
	Chest	Now breathe in... and as you breathe out, imagine that all the bones in the upper half of your body have turned to butter, soft and limp...	
	Relax everything	And one more time... breathe in... and as you breathe out... let all of the muscles in the whole of your body relax... let them go completely to rest... imagine that your arms and legs feel heavy and tired... imagine that the whole of your body feels heavy and tired... like cement... your arms and legs feel like cement... the whole of your body feels like a dead weight... so heavy and tired... imagine that your toes and feet are relaxing... imagine that all the muscles around your face are relaxed now... and you can forget all about those arms and legs...	
3		***Begin the mental relaxation***	
		I wonder if you can imagine a suburb outside a city somewhere... at night... with lots of houses going down a hillside... and all the lights are on... and there are cars in the streets...	
	Lights out	And now imagine... with each gentle breath out... the lights in those houses at the top of that hillside going out... and the cars slowing down... and with each breath out... more lights go out in houses further down... cars are slowing down... everything gradually becoming dark and quiet... and on the next breath... everything closing down... relaxing now... until all the lights have gone out... and the whole hillside is dark... the cars stopped... and everything is calm and peaceful... dark and quiet...	

Direct Hypnotic Gaze Induction

The Hypnotic Gaze induction script is a spectacular showy induction. Use of the Hypnotic Gaze induction is what started the belief that hypnosis must be some secret black art that gives you power over people. You actually can make people go into trance just by looking into their eyes.

In fact it is based on physiology. When people look at you with an intense stare your mind is likely to interpret this as a threat. If the stare continues your mind will start to go into fight or flight mode and your unconscious mind takes control. If you don't focus on their eyes they cannot stare back, and they get disconcerted. This starts a cascade of internal responses that you can hijack.

There is only one type of hypnosis, but many ways to get there. The Hypnotic Gaze induction is actually a variation of the Instant Induction using the startle reflex.

	You should have the other person standing facing you, about arms length from you.		The Set Up
	Look into their eyes. Keep your eyes on their eyes all time. Just look into their eyes as if you are curious, as if you looking for some reaction deep inside that you know will be coming.		Start the process of unnerving them
	Reach out both arms and touch the person lightly on the outside of their shoulders.		Unexpected action
	Lower your arms.		odd action
	Lift up your arms again and place the palms of your hands against the outsides of their shoulders, on the upper arms.		More unexpected actions
	Press once, gently.		Start them wondering
	Press again, more firmly. Do not say anything. Keep looking into their eyes all the while.		They will start being uneasy
	Keeping your hand where they are, nod very slightly to yourself, as if you are satisfied with		Mysterious knowledge

	something.	
	Press your hands against their shoulders more firmly now. Keep the pressure on.	Urgency
	Look into their eyes. You are not examining their eyeballs: look at the bridge of their nose, otherwise you will get into a staring contest. You are giving the impression of looking into and through their eyes but your focus is actually somewhere inside their head, or beyond them. (You might have to practice this in a mirror).	Look THROUGH them
	At some point, the eyes of the other person will begin to do one of two things. The eyes will either widen and show fear and uncertainty - you will see this with your peripheral vision - or they will begin to glaze over and lose focus.	Watch for the reaction
	Now you can do several different things to cause hypnosis:	
	a) if they show fear and uncertainty	
	they are going into fight or flight mode. The slightest stimulus will knock them out.	
	You can swing your hand in front of their eyes and snap your fingers. The sudden noise and movement will invoke the startle response and they will go into trance. You must then take charge and tell them what to do instantly, or they will come out again.	SNAP!
	Or	
	You can pull them towards you with your hands, firmly but gently, off balance, and say the word 'sleep' in a commanding voice. The sudden movement and command will put them into trance. Then start telling them what to do.	No hard movement - safety!
	b) If you see their eyes glaze and they get a 'lost' look	
	They are retreating into trance to get safe, and any command will be obeyed.	
	Begin to rock them back and forth, gently. Get them swaying. If they look as if they are going into trance pull them forward against your body and hold them up. Say the word 'sleep' into their ear so no one else hears. It looks very showy.	

	Or		
	If they are not ready for trance, tell them that every movement is making them more relaxed and going deeper. Keep up with the gentle swaying and a soothing repetitive voice until they go into trance. Then continue with what you want them to do.		
	Whatever way you use, the easiest thing to do is to lift up their arm and tell them it will stay there, weightless, until you tell them to lower it.		
	Then address your audience and continue with the demonstration.		

Dave Mason © 2011 www.key-hypnosis.com

Visualization Inductions

Cloud visualization induction

The Drifting Cloud induction script is a combined visualization and Countdown Hypnotic Induction. It works by relaxing the mind, then getting the client to remember a time when they were relaxing on a beach. The experience of the beach is used to lead in to visualizing one cloud, then more clouds, then watching each cloud slowly drift away and disappear. As the visualization progresses suggestions of getting smaller, more distant, darker are used to pace and lead with the breathing. Very effective.

	Cloud hypnotic Induction script		
	So settle back now, think about how comfortable you can become... and close your eyes...		Bind = how
Relax the body	Now take a deep breath, and hold it... and ... just let it all go... ahhhh... That's good...		Start releasing tension
	When you are ready... take another deep breath.... and as you do... tense all your muscles... and then as you breath out... let everything get loose and relaxed.		Let go muscle tension
	And as you breath out... think about being outdoors somewhere...		Bind
	and maybe you can imagine lying on a beach... the kind of beach you like... somewhere... on a warm day... nothing to do... and no one to bother you... waves rolling gently... just lying there... completely at ease... and in the distance there is the sound of things happening... and the smells of holiday... while you lie there... head back... shoulders relaxed... feeling totally at peace...	V	Invoking memories with sound, smell, vision.
	And in the sky... high above... in the blue sky... there are clouds...		
	and as you watch the clouds drift across... and the clouds are drifting slowly from one side to the other...	V	
	And those clouds go down towards the horizon...	V	Pace with

and as they go... you watch them... gently floating... and you count the clouds going by...		breathing... Count down deepener
and as they go off there are ten left... and then one disappears...		
and there are nine...		
and still the clouds go down and there's eight...		
and now there's seven...		
and then there's six...		
and those clouds are drifting gently down...and five...		
and four...		
and with each cloud disappearing... you feel more and more relaxed... more at ease...		
and everything is becoming calm... and relaxed... and as you go deeper things are becoming darker, peaceful... and breathing slowly, gently... relaxing deeper and deeper...		
and three...		
and two...		
and there's just one cloud left... and you can imagine yourself in that cloud... being completely surrounded by a lovely soft warm fleecy cloud...	V	
and you can feel yourself... gently supported..... floating, drifting... just going down and down and down ... as if you were floating like that cloud... safe and secure...	D	
letting go as that last cloud disappears...	I	

Dave Mason © 2009 www.key-hypnosis.com

The Blackboard Induction

The 'Wipe out the letters Induction' is an example of how to use visualisation as the basis of induction.

Procedure: This induction uses the common device of writing letters on a blackboard and then wiping them off again.

Method: It works in two ways. Part of it is self hypnosis, suggesting that as each letter is wiped off the listener feels more relaxed. Part of it is direct suggestion, suggesting that the more letters are written the harder it gets to remember the next letter.

Advantage: The advantage of this type of induction is that it allows the listener to relax at their own pace, and has many more stages than the 'one to ten' countdown induction.

Uses: General purpose induction

Extensions: Once you understand the principle of the metaphor method you will be able to do inductions based on any kind of visual changes, leaves dropping off trees, lights going out, clouds in the sky dissolving, etc. It is the basis of the old advice of counting sheep jumping over a fence to get to sleep.

	Wiping away consciousness		
	Take a deep breath... and let it go... Ahhh... That's right...		encouragement
	Now take another deep breath... that's good....		pace the client
	Now just allow your eyes to close... that's very good...		
	[add instructions here for loosening the shoulders...etc if you think it is needed]		Physical relaxation
Memory	I wonder if you have ever written letters on a blackboard at school... or maybe on a whiteboard... or maybe you remember writing letters on the sand and letting the sea wash them away... or seen clouds in the sky that look like one thing and then change into something else...	V	Always offer a choice of possible ways to form the letters.
Capability	There are many ways that you can form letters...	D	Seeding
	And now I would like you to think of something you can write letters on... a blackboard or a big blue sky... whatever you want....		let the client choose

	And I want you to imagine writing the letter 'A' there... and then just imagine wiping away the letter 'A'...	V	
	and then imagine the letter 'B'... and then just imagine letter 'B' being wiped away... disappearing... in any way that makes sense to you...	V	allow the client to choose
	and keep on thinking of the next letter... and as you wipe away the next letter... you can feel yourself... loosening... relaxing... getting more and more comfortable... letting go...	>	disappearing = relaxing
	and as each letter disappears you can become more and more relaxed... more at ease...	>	
	And you can continue putting the letters there... and fading out... and getting more comfortable...	>	who is 'fading'?
	and as you relax more and more... it becomes too much trouble to think of the next letter...	D	amnesia
	and when you get to that stage you can just relax completely...	I	'when' bind
	allow your mind to drift away... to a place where there is nothing to think about... nothing to worry you... relaxed and peaceful and calm...	V	Dissociation
	and take a few moments now and allow that lovely feeling of relaxation to spread... as you go deeper and deeper....	I	bind 'as you...' inevitability
	[either do a deepener, or your convincer and then carry on with the therapy]		
		I	

David Mason   www.key-hypnosis.com © 2010

Candle visualization induction

This short hypnosis induction uses the association between flames and heat, between flames and night time, between heat and night and getting ready to drift off into sleep. The hypnotic induction is suitable for both visual and kinesthetic clients. Everyone has watched a candle flame at some point, everyone can remember snuggling down on a winter evening and feeling warm and safe, so everyone can relate to this hypnosis induction.

	I wonder if you can imagine a flame... a single candle flame... a small flame burning in the dark...	V	Candle
	and that candle flame giving off a soft light... gently glowing in the dark... a symbol of safe, cosy, happy feelings...	=	
Memory	and remembering a time when there was a candle... and watching the flame... and losing your thoughts as you watch that flame...		
	and imagine that candle flame now getting smaller and smaller ... and as that gets smaller allow your eyes to close... and relax..	>	
	and now imagine another flame... a fire burning quietly in a hearth somewhere... in a fireplace... and its night time...and the flames are flickering and weaving patterns of soft light...		Indoor hearth
	and imagine all around... just out of sight... a room... warm and cozy and comfortable... the sort of room where you can relax in a big chair and watch the flre light flickering... with your eyes closed... and feeling so relaxed... safe and warm... imagine what it would be like in that room... lying back... with the fire glowing... and gradually getting darker and darker... and more peaceful... and you arms and legs getting heavy... imagine them tired and heavy... and as you relax deeper now... the room fades away... to a soft smooth darkness all round...		physical metaphor
	and in that darkness... imagine a single point of light... on a dark night... far away... long, long ago... the light of a camp fire... and people around that camp fire... and all around the dark night... quiet and		outdoor campfire

	calm and peaceful... and the fading flow of that camp fire...feeling the gentle warmth... snuggled down in some soft fleecy covering... relaxed... surrounded by your people... safe and secure... warm and comfortable...	
	and as that campfire slowly gets smaller and smaller... and everything settling down... deeper and deeper... relaxing more and more...	
	going to rest... in that place... far away... in that velvety darkness... sinking down and down... and your mind drifting away... nothing to do... nothing to think about... empty and relaxed...	Trance achieved
	[Now do a depth test or continue with the therapy part]	

David Mason   www.key-hypnosis.com © 2010

Falling Shadows Induction

Description: The induction script is followed by a metaphor of going to sleep that acts as a gentle relaxing deepener.

Principle: The deepener works by invoking images of little animals snuggling down and this connects to childhood memories of feeling relaxed and sleepy when you feel warm and safe.

Advantages: Nice and soft slow relaxation that you can pace with the client's breathing.

Disadvantages: Make sure your client is comfortable with ideas of darkness and countryside, and has no negative memories to do with bedtime.

Uses: Just a nice change from the standard deepener for people who say they like going to the country to relax.

Extensions: You can move the action anywhere that has a special meaning for the client, vary it to a desert scene, etc.

INDUCTION SECTION

	Standard induction		
	So settle back now, get comfortable... and close your eyes....		
	Now take a deep breath, and hold it... and... just let it all go... ahhhh...That's good...		Start releasing tension
	When you are ready... take another deep breath..... and as you do... lift your shoulders up... and as you breath out... let them slump down and relax.		Let go muscle tension
	Now lift your arms slightly... and on the next breath out... let them drop back naturally... and relax your whole body		Let go muscle tension
	And I wonder if you could imagine what it would be like if your arms and legs had become so heavy ... that you just could not move them... that they felt as if they were made of lead...	D	Dissociation
	...and just allow that heaviness to grow		
	... and now I would like you to focus on your breathing... just become aware of the gentle in and out of your breath...	D	Dissociation
	And as you think about your breathing... with	I	Dissociation

each breath out... just allow your body to relax more...		
and you could become curious as to exactly how relaxed you can be...		
...and focusing on each breath out will let you relax and settle down a little deeper... each time you breathe out...		Deepening
...while you think about that...		Ambiguity
and a little more relaxation after every breath... that's good...	D	Deepening
and continue breathing gently... relaxing...		
And as an experiment, for the next ten breaths... you could start counting each breath out... counting down from ten down to one... as you breathe out... say the next number under your breath... or think of the next number... if you can...	I	Deepening
allowing each breath to relax you more... and as you relax completely ...as you say each number quietly to yourself... you might find that those numbers are disappearing...you may find it harder and harder to know what number comes next... and you can relax those numbers away... if you want to... those numbers can just disappear completely... with each gentle breath... as you drift down and down...	I	Make the listener aware that they are in trance now
And as you become aware of that at some level... that means that things are going exactly the way they should be...		Reassurance
... and your mind is opening to new possibilities...	D	Seeding

DEEPENER SECTION

Falling shadows deepener		
Now imagine somewhere in the countryside... it's getting near dusk... the sun going down behind some clouds... and all around in the gathering darkness... are trees and fields and streams... and little cottages... warm golden light from the windows...	V	Dissociation

	and inside the cottage... a open fire warms the room... and there is a comfortable seat... with soft cushions...		
	and imagine what it would be like to relax in that seat... as the fire crackles quietly... and outside the sun slips away and darkness falls softly like a leaf flutters down from a tree...	M	deepening darkness = trance
	and as you relax there... imagine the darkness gathering outside... flowers closing... insects folding their wings... birds settling down in their nests... everything settling down for the night...	M	closing down
	and you can snuggle down too... breathing gently... relaxing more and more... and as the darkness outside gets deeper and deeper... you are relaxing more and more...	>	darkness = trance
	and outside ... inside a hollow tree... safe and warm... a family of soft furry creatures... are settling down for the night... cozy and comfortable... wrapped in silky soft fur... drowsy and dreamy...	M	snuggling deeper
	nothing to think about... forgetting about the day... the place... enjoying warmth and calm and letting go completely...		dissociation
	that's right... and take a few moments and enjoy that....		allow time to deepen

Dave Mason © 2009 www.key-hypnosis.com

The Swirling Paper induction

The Swirling Paper Induction is my version of the falling leaf induction.

Procedure: It works by suggesting dissociation into a familiar snuggly place, and then visualising and pacing a bit of paper being picked up and drifting down and down.

Advantages: It is simple to visualise so works with poor visualisers. Hypervigilant people find the imagery easy to follow and non-threatening. It is better to use paper rather than the traditional leaf. People find it hard to decide what type of leaf to use or to visualise a particular leaf. Paper is much simpler.

Disadvantages: Best used after another induction

Uses: I tag it on to the end of the induction if I think there is any doubt at all about whether the client is fully in trance. Then test with a finger lift.

Target	Induction text	Comments
	[Start after the eyes are closed]	
	And as you are lying there... eyes closed... muscles relaxing... hearing these words...	Pacing
	you can experience many things... and my voice can become the voice of anyone you want it to be... the voice of a teacher... the voice of a friend... something from long ago... *[Erickson taught this technique to dissociate away from the therapist's presence in the here and now]*	Visualisation
	My voice can become the sound of rain on the roof.. or the sound of a branch tapping on the window sill on a winter's night...	Dissociation
Memory	While you are curled up snug in a warm bed... feeling safe and secure and relaxed... knowing that everything is OK...	suggestion of settling down
	and I wonder if you can imagine an empty street somewhere... and the wind blowing along that empty street...	Visualisation
	and as the wind blows along it picks up a bit of paper... tumbling along the street... and then that wind picks up the bit of paper... lifts it and drops it ... and lifts it and drops it...	
	and the wind picks up the paper... carries it... safe and secure... swirling whirling around... carries it up into the air... higher and higher... away from	

	this place... and that peice of paper twists and turns... rolls and rotates... and the wind carries it ever higher... safe, supported...	
	and then the wind begins to let that paper down... and you can feel that paper moving left and right... to right and left ... and left and right... and that's left is to be right.. and right to the left ... that's right... it's right to be right and what's left is left... then that's right again to be left on the right...	Confusion technique
	... and fluttering down and round... swirling swooping falling... going down and down... deeper and deeper... floating swirling turning...	suggestion of detachment
	and the paper lands gently on a little stream... and the stream carries it along on the surface... bobbing this way and that... round and round... gliding past rocks and rapids... and always it is going down... until it comes to a deep pool...	Metaphor for going into trance
	and the paper begins to sink down... and down... deep into that water... until it snuggles safe and secure and rests on the bottom... waiting... calm and relaxed... completely letting go... lying there gently...	muscle relaxation
	and the paper flattens out smooth and soft...	
	and everything is quiet and peaceful... just lying there... loose and limp... open to any current that comes along... completely at ease...	
	That's good...	Reassurance
	Depth test	
	and as you are lying there... breathing gently... hearing these words... you might become aware of a need, a feeling... a compulsion... in your hands... a need to move a finger or a thumb... and it might start as a tiny tremor... and just let it happen the way it wants to... do not assist in any way... it will just happen.... now... as soon as you are ready...	
	and when that moves we will continue.	

Dave Mason © 2009 www.key-hypnosis.com

Butterfly Hypnosis Induction

This gentle relaxation visualization uses an image of tired butterfly and repeated images of down, and resting, and letting go to create a gentle relaxation hypnotic induction.

The Butterfly Hypnosis Induction is an example of how to use visualization to do simple hypnotic induction. The Butterfly hypnosis induction uses the technique of linking relaxation to some physical movement.

Metaphor visualization inductions take advantage of the mind's built-in ability to see connections between two quite different things. This is the essence of metaphor. Visualize something, imagine it changing and imagine yourself changing at the same time. Many hypnotic inductions depend on metaphor, leaves falling, lights going dim, walking down steps, and suggesting that as these things are going down, the listener can relax too. And the more it goes down, the deeper the listener can relax.

	Butterfly Induction		
	Take a moment now... and prepare yourself to relax... shrug your shoulders ... lift and drop your arms... tense the muscles of your legs and then relax them...		Muscular relaxation
	Now close your eyes... imagine that all the muscles of your face are relaxing... imagine that your eyes are totally relaxed...		Close the eyes
	now breath out and really relax... and become aware of how heavy your arms and legs are... feel the weight of your body pressing down... allow that feeling to grow... feeling heavier and heavier... totally relaxed...		relaxation
	Now imagine a place far away from here...		Dissociation
	a place somewhere outdoors... a forest clearing... or somewhere in the country... imagine a day in summer... exactly the kind of day you like...	V	set the scene
Memory	a day when you just feel like lying back and relaxing... imagine somewhere where you can relax... lying or sitting comfortably... at ease	V	

bring to mind a place of peace and calm... scents of outdoors... the air clear and still..		
and in that air... things moving... fluttering... dancing about in the sunlight ...bright points of color... and as you watch more and more are there...	V	
all around... clouds of butterflies... rising and falling... flying this way and that... happy to be there in the sunlight...	V	
and then... as if there was some silent signal...		
those clouds of butterflies begin to rotate... to swirl this way and that... changing direction... moving all together... first rising up.. and then spiralling downwards... down and down...		
and the image fades... and everything goes quiet...		
And as you watch... one butterfly ... tired and wanting to rest... slowly spirals down... dropping gently like a leaf softly floating on the air	M	
and as it floats gently down... you feel yourself drifting... gently... down... more relaxed.. more at ease... settling down	M	
And that one butterfly... resting quietly now... and as you watch... that butterfly moves its wings... slowly... and as it lowers those wings slowly down... letting those wings relax and droop and flatten... you feel yourself breathing out.. exhaling... relaxing... letting go... feeling heavier and heavier... more relaxed...		Fractionation 1
and again that butterfly tries to raise its wings and then gently feels them sink down... as if too tired to hold them up... and as those wings drop down again... you can relax deeper... deeper and deeper... just like those wings... loose and soft...		Fractionation 2
and once more those wings rise a little and this time they droop all the way down... lying loose and relaxed... completely limp and soft and comfortable...		Fractionation 3
and the light is getting soft and diffuse... everything going out of focus...	V	

	and you feel lighter... drifting away now...		
	like that butterfly... relaxing now... down and down...	M	
	allow your mind to drift away... to a place where there is nothing to think about... nothing to worry you... relaxed and peaceful and calm...	V	Dissociation
	and take a few moments now and allow that lovely feeling of relaxation to spread... as you go deeper and deeper....	I	bind 'as you...' inevitability
	[either do a deepener, or a convincer and then carry on with the therapy]		

Dave Mason © 2009 www.key-hypnosis.com

Personalized Hypnotic Induction Script

A tailored induction is a type of script that allows the person to choose what hypnotic images they prefer. The induction will work for first time hypnosis but it is better to use it where the person already has some experience of going into trance.

This script shows how the hypnotist asks the client what images or visualization works for them when going into trace, and builds an induction around that.

In this case the client asked for something in the countryside near a waterfall, so those elements were woven into the induction. You can use the same technique for anything that the client likes.

	Personalized hypnotic Induction script		
	Are you comfortable? So settle back now, think about how quickly you can go into trance... and close your eyes...		Bind = how quickly?
	Take a deep breath... and relax...		
	And how would you like to go into hypnosis? What would be a nice way of leading you in?		Find favourite way into trance
	Client: I quite like going to a place you really like. And being safe... and secure... and... a nice little beach or... a park... or in the bush...		
	And when you are there... what kind of movement or change around you would be nice for you to link to suggestions of going down into trance?		
	Client: Maybe just in a little place... like by a waterfall... somewhere private... some place with the sun coming through.. and just the water...		
	How about the sun going down and getting darker and darker?		false start
	Client: No, I like the sun... just watching the water eddying down would be good...		
	All right... now take another deep breath... and one more deep breath... that's right ...		Relax the body
	just shrug your shoulders down... rub the whole of your face... get rid of all the tension in your face... rub your forehead and your eyes and your		Rub out all the tension in a distressed client

	cheeks...		
	now, hands flat on your thighs... and as you are lying there... breathing gently, relaxing... hearing the sound of my voice...		pacing and leading
	you can imagine, perhaps... being in some place somewhere... somewhere you like to go and relax... and this can be a real place or somewhere you might want to imagine... it can be on a beach or in the country... it could be in a garden... it could be anywhere you like...	V	repeat the client's likes back to them. give all possible options
	outdoors... perhaps by a waterfall...		preferred place
	the sort of place where you feel safe and secure... someplace where the sun is shining and you can relax...		repeat clien't specifications
Memory	and just imagine how it would be... to be in that place		link to memories
	and you can imagine lying on the grass perhaps... on a comfortable seat of some sort... perhaps on grassy bank... listening to the sound of a waterfall... as the water splashes down...	K	start leading the client
	and allow yourself to think of how lovely it would be ... just be in that place... nothing to think about... nothing to do... no cares at all...	K	link to the feeling
	imagine lying relaxing... just become aware of all the muscles relaxing... your shoulders relaxing... all the muscles in your upper arms relaxing... your forearms relaxing and your hands relaxing... imagine the feel of the support under your back... as your chest relaxes... and you tummy relaxes... your hips are relaxing and the weight of your legs and arms...	I	brief progressive muscle relaxation
	and imagine the feel of the sun on your face... warm and comfortable... and feeling so safe and secure... like a place where you could just snuggle up and be quiet... calm	K	Kinesthetic feelings of safety
	And allow your mind to drift across to where that water is flowing nearby... and imagine that water as a series of pools... and the water gently flowing from one pool to the next... as the water goes down and down...	I	
	Now imagine in the top pool... a swirling,	K	

	eddying as the water begins to flow... and it goes down into the next pool.. and there the water is still and dark... deep.. and in your mind feel that water gently slide down into the next pool... and as it goes that water is swirling... round and round and the current is taking it down... and down... and it gently flows deeper and deeper into another pool... and there the water swirls round and down and imagine following that water current down and down deeper and deeper... drifting floating... and that water goes down into another deep silent pool		
	and imagine yourself drifting with that water... flowing softly deeper and deeper down and down... letting yourself drifting along... being carried like a leaf this way and that... swirling... spinning... floating... drifting down now... sinking into a comfortable state as that water takes you deeper and deeper... and you experience that deeper and deeper you can become even more relaxed... just letting the water take it all away... gently drifting... and imagine that leaf... finally drifting down deeper still waters flowing... settling gently somewhere... safe and secure... completely relaxed... at ease with the world...	M	Leaf metaphor
	and as that water flows away... you can allow your mind to flow away... drift off somewhere... nothing matters...	D	Trance achieved
	[Now do a depth test or continue with the therapy part]		

Dave Mason © 2010 www.key-hypnosis.com

Emotional Release Induction

The Emotional Release Hypnosis Induction is a specialised induction that is used in clinical hypnotherapy. This kind of induction introduces elements of the visualization metaphor that are later used in the main therapy session.

In this induction the client is asked to imagine a spark of light and lets that spark lead them down a corridor that takes them deeper and deeper. The corridor then become the main element that leads to the place where the client will make the emotional changes they need.

The induction is multilayered and used Kinesthetic suggestion, visual suggestions, auditory suggestions and metaphor imagery to put the person into trance.

	Emotional Release induction script		
	Good... that's good... and now take a deep breath... ahhhh... and another deep breath... and one more deep breath... and just allow the whole of your body to relax... that's good		
Resources	Now that you are relaxing... you can allow your mind to change things for you... you can use the inner power that is in all of us...		Pre-supposition
	and I want you to imagine that inner power... and just for a moment allow your eyes to close.. that's right...	V	start the induction
	and as you lie there... relaxing... I wonder if you can imagine some dark dim place somewhere... some place safe and warm and comfortable...	V	pacing
	and imagine there is a speck of light... and imagine that speck of light moving... and imagine that speck of light guiding you safely down... and down... and as that speck of light moves you feel yourself drawn down and down...		guide into trance
	and thinking about that speck of light... you can feel your body slowing down... your eyes getting heavy... and the weight of your arms and legs... feel your arms and legs getting tired	K	kinaesthetic induction

	and heavy... imagine the whole of your body getting heavy and tired... and relaxing... deeper and deeper now...	V	
	imagine going deeper into that dark place... as that speck leads you on... gliding further down... imagine your body sinking... drifting... deeper and deeper...	K	kinaesthetic induction
	and feel yourself relaxing... easing... sinking... like going down into the deep dark blue waters of the ocean...		
	feel yourself slowly, gently... following that speck... deeper and deeper... more and more relaxed... and imagine that speck of light is leading you through a long dim corridor... and as you go down that corridor...	V	visualization induction
	every sound you hear makes you even more relaxed... allows you to drift even deeper... and all around you... things are becoming quiet and peaceful... and every sound becomes soothing and gentle and every sound is leading you down and down as you relax those sounds right out of your mind... everything is disappearing...	A	sound induction
	and just thinking about that speck of light... imagine it now spreading soft gentle light everywhere... feel yourself wrapped in that light... cocooned... held gently safely... drifting away... supported by that light...		
	soft and indistinct... like a quiet glow... as it softly spreads out further and further... you feel yourself somehow spreading... easing... letting go... feel yourself going deeper and with each passing moment...	M	metaphor induction
	the feeling comes over you that nothing really matters now... as you relax more and more deeply... you feel that you don't really care any more... just letting everything go...	K	relaxing
	and as you go deeper... just imagine the tiny muscles of your eyes... becoming so relaxed... so relaxed... it's as if you just can't open those eyes... as if those eyes are glued tight shut... and you just cannot open your eyes...		Depth test

	and just feel those eyes relaxing completely... letting go... deeper and deeper... that's right... [do a depth test]		

Dave Mason © 2010 www.key-hypnosis.com

Dark River Induction

A visualization and breathing induction based images of floating down a river into darkness.

	Visualization Induction		
	I wonder if you can imagine a river... a wide dark silent river... now lie back... close your eyes... and think of that river...		Dissociation
	and it's almost night... and the river is flowing through a city...and city is bright with lights... and there's traffic about ... and just imagine...if you can... that you are floating safe and secure on that river...		Metaphor
	and with each breath out that river flows a little further... and as it flows past... the lights along the riverbank begin to go out... and the traffic begins to slow down...		
	and with each breath... as you breathe out... you can sense the river flowing down, and more city lights go out...		
	and as the river flows on the darkness slowly spreads across the city... city becoming dark... and the traffic slows and stops...		
	and still the river flows on... quiet, gentle, strong... flowing through that city and as it passes more and more lights go out... until the whole city is dark... and gently breathing... the river flows on... through a darkened countryside... calm and peaceful... flowing down to toward a distant sea... far away... where dark waters merge and mingle... gently carrying you... holding you ... and that river spreads out into the warm welcoming darkness and you can just be carried wherever it flows...		Pace with breathing
	That's right... and you can just enjoy that feeling of relaxation and just allow your mind to drift off... into a comfortable... dark... warm place...		Dissociation
	that's good, you're doing very well...		Reassurance
	and you can remember this feeling of relaxation and ease and comfort ... and any time you want to...		Dissociation

	you can go into this state... by breathing gently... imagining relaxing and floating down that dark river...	
	Just allow yourself to go deeper and deeper now ... and each comfortable breath out... takes you deeper and deeper... more relaxed... more at ease...	Pace with breathing
	That's very good ... you're doing very well...	Reassurance

Dave Mason © 2011 www.key-hypnosis.com

Rainy Day Induction

This induction uses the common memory of a rainy day to link going into trance to a visualization of raindrops running down a window pane. Then the script creates a deepener from a memory of being in a car and uses the rhythmic swish of the wipers to induce a hypnotic trance. It is a pace and lead induction, so you need to be confident of your voice control, and it is essential that you are able to time it to their breathing. Use as a lead in to any sort of journey metaphor.

	Induction Section		
	Are you ready to go into trance?		
	Good, then let's begin.		
	Now settle down... and prepare to go on a journey... a journey of the mind...		
	That's good. Now just wiggle around in the chair and get really comfortable...		relax the body
Memory	I wonder if you remember a time long ago when it was raining?... remember at time when you were somewhere looking out at the rain falling... imagine now... rain on the grass... seeping into the earth... and rain on the window... and looking at the rain forming little trails on the window... as the water slowly runs down... little drops forming little rivers... stopping and starting...	V	Dissociation
	Now just close your eyes... and imagine that rainy day... with raindrops running down the window pane...	V	
	imagine following one drop as it goes down the window... and imagine that every time you breath out... that drop rolls down a bit further...	>	pace with breathing
	and as it rolls down... you feel yourself getting more relaxed...	D	
	and then with the next breath... that drop rolls down a little more... and you feel your yourself going down... relaxing a little more...		
	and focus on your breathing... let every breath take you down... imagine with each breath more raindrops slowly trickling down... watching raindrop after raindrop going down ... joining and		

merging... and going down gets easier and easier...		
Automobile deepener		
and as you are relaxing there now... think of another time... in the passenger seat of a car... looking through the front window of a car... ... and watch the raindrops on the glass... and then the gentle swish of the wipers as they clear away the rain...		
and feel yourself relaxing now... settling down in the passenger seat... each swish of the wipers making you feel more relaxed and sleepy now...	>	
and with each breath imagine those wipers sweeping away the raindrops... and with each breath those wipers are wiping all your stress, all the tension... is getting wiped away now... relaxed and comfortable...		Pace with breathing
each stroke is wiping out everything and then taking you deeper... wiping away and taking you deeper.		Pace with breathing
and the heater is on...and you remember being warm and drowsy... the swish of the wipers and the thrum of the tires making you more tired...		
and let that feeling take over now... allow yourself to go deeper and deeper... imagine being carried along... nothing to do, nothing to worry about... time to just let go and allow things to carry you along...		
and every sound you hear takes you deeper... and each breath is making you more comfortable, more relaxed... more at ease...		
That's right...		
[do a depth test]		

Turning the candles out induction

An effective lead in to regression therapy

Candles have always been associated with hypnosis. One of the earliest inductions was by James Braid, who hypnotized someone at a dinner party by asking them to stare at a candle flame.

This Candle induction depends on the more modern idea that candles are used as an aid to meditation and relaxation, not for illumination.

Turning out candles is gentle way to lead someone into trance.

Candle Hypnosis Induction		
Take a deep breath.		
Take another deep breath and let your eyes close.		
and one more breath... and as you breath out... you can let it all go...		Breathing induction
That's right. And now imagine that your whole body is relaxing... feel your arms getting heavy... your legs feeling heavy... your whole body is getting heavy... loose and soft and heavy...	D	Kinesthetic induction
and your eyes are getting heavy...		
and imagine you are in a room somewhere... dim and quiet...	V	
and it is soft and warm and comfortable there... and there are candles shining softly all around... many many candles...		
and now imagine that with each breath out... as you relax... a candle goes out...		
and on the next breath... another candle goes out... and then with every gentle breath out ... more and more candles go out... and you can imagine that room getting dim and dark... dim and dark and quiet and peaceful...		Candle Visualization induction
until all those candles have gone out... and you are totally relaxed... totally at ease... [Pause]	D	
[Now do an eye catalepsy test]		Test for trance

Dave Mason © 2011 www.key-hypnosis.com

Kinaesthetic Inductions

Name the Colours Induction

This is an unusual induction based on awareness of feelings in the body. It is one of those inductions that is more complicated to explain than it is to do.

Principle: It works by by-passing the analytical mind and dealing directly with feelings and associations. While the mind is focussing on bodily experiences it slips in additional suggestions of relaxation and comfort and letting go. Because it is bodily based, there is nothing for the analytical mind to challenge.

Use: It is good for clients who are nervous about the whole hypnosis process since it lets them go at their own pace.

Advantage: you get continuous feedback that lets you know what the client is experiencing during every step.

Disadvantages: Clients need to be comfortable with paying attention to their feelings. A few clients coming to therapy for the first time are so inwardly agitated that they stay in a state of alarm until you deal with it, and in order to stay alert to threats will tell you they don't feel anything. Use a confusion or relaxation induction with those clients.

Extensions: There is nothing special about using colours. You could use just about anything else that will have emotional associations for the particular client – flowers, places, their children, musical instruments etc.

	Dialogue		Comments
	Are you ready to go into trance?	I	Seeding the idea
	... and you are always in control... anytime you feel you are not comfortable about anything at all... just say the word... 'wait' . OK?		Safety
	Feeling comfortable?	I	3rd Yes set
	I want you to feel totally comfortable when you are in trance... so if want to move that's OK, and when you move you can become even more comfortable...	>	Pre-suppositions
Capability	The only thing you need to do to go into hypnosis is wanting to be hypnotised. If	>	Inevitability

	you decide you want to, trance will follow. Nothing can stop the process once you have decided you want it to happen now.		
Behaviour	And the funny thing is, you don't have to do anything... You don't know how you make it happen, but you will know that it is happening when it starts happening... you just have to let it happen all on its own...		
	Like watching a sunset... you just watch as it goes down, the sky getting deeper and deeper and as you relax more... the stars magically appear	V	Metaphor
	I am going to name a colour, and when I say that colour you can become aware of a change happening in you ... most people get a warm feeling in the chest... or maybe for you it will be somewhere else... but you get a warm and comforting feeling... it will remind you of times you felt good...		
	When you get that feeling... let me know... and we will go on...		
	And then I will say a different colour and you can say when you are getting the feeling of that colour... and each feeling will make you more comfortable... more relaxed...		
	When I say the colour don't think about it, just start opening up to the feeling, become aware of the feeling and let it happen... So, are you ready for the first colour now?		
	[Wait for agreement or objection]		
	Purple [Snap!] *Say a colour and snap your fingers or touch their wrist.*		
	[Wait for them to say what they are feeling].		
	[When they report a feeling...] 'That's right... And it feels good, warm and comforting, isn't it?	I	

	[Encourage them to focus on their inner feelings, on what they are experiencing in their body.		
	When you hear the next colour, that good feeling you have will spread and you will feel yourself relaxing more... and as the feeling spread you will find your eyes wanting to relax... you can close them now or later... it really doesn't matter...	I	
	Now - nod if you are ready for another colour		
	Blue [Snap!] *Say a different colour and snap your fingers or touch their wrist.*		
	[Wait for the client to express their feeling, or see the eyes closing]		
	OK, that's good - nod when are you ready for the next colour		Reassurance
	When you hear the next colour you will focus your attention on your eyes. The feeling from that colour will make those eyes so relaxed so tired that they will feel as if they are stuck together. You just will not be able to open those eyes.	D	
	Green [Snap!] *Say another colour and snap your fingers or touch their wrist.*		
	Now just feel those eyes relax all the way and imagine that you just cannot open them. And when you are sure that they are relaxed all the way down...and they just will not open... you can try to open them and you will find that they just will not open. And the harder you try, the harder they stick shut. You just cannot open those eyes.	D	Eye Catalepsy
	[watch for signs of eye catalepsy. If you get it then the induction is finished and you go on with whatever therapy you had in mind]		
	[If the eyes open then say] That's good. Your eyes are getting ready to relax even deeper. Now in a moment I am		Switch to Fractionation

	going to ask you to close your eyes again. Then I will ask you to open them and you will find it more difficult to get them to open. Then I will ask you to try to open them again, and it will be more difficult still, you might be able to open them a little or maybe not, and then I will ask again and you will find your eyes so relaxed that they just will not open.		
	Now close your eyes and when you feel them relaxing deeper and deeper you can try to open them. And each time you relax those eyes you will feel yourself drifting deeper and deeper into trance.		
	[Continue until the fractionation works]		

Dave Mason © 2009 www.key-hypnosis.com

Kinesthetic Induction

Some people find it easy to visualize, and others don't, so some people do not respond to the Staircase hypnosis induction script. There is nothing wrong with the staircase induction method, but no hypnotic scripts work on everyone. The problem is that many people are kinaesthetic - they can't visualize, they have to imagine that they are holding something in their hands or feeling things pressing on their body. This is quite normal, about ten percent of the population experience the world this way. To hypnotize kinesthetic learners you need to use a kinesthetic induction.

For people who who can't visualize, any visualization method will be difficult. Hypnotic scripts should never use suggestions like '*there is a wide pink marble stair in front of you, with polished wooden handrails and blue curtains*'... etc. The more specific it is the less likely people will be able to visualize it.

With a kinesthetic learner you need a different type of hypnosis script - a special kinesthetic script where there is no need to visualize anything. Kinesthetic people respond to suggestions of movement, pressure, weight, spinning, holding, feeling so this kinesthetic hypnotic induction script is written using kinesthetic principles.

	Now before you go into trance easily it is best to make sure that your body is completely at ease.	Bind
	Relaxation Induction	
	So **shrug your shoulders** and let them drop.	
	Now **lift** your arms and let them **drop**.	
	Become **aware of the weight** of those arms as you let them relax completely.	I dissociation
	Now **tense** the muscles in your thighs and let them **release**. **Feel** your legs relaxing.	I
	Now **tense** the muscles in your calves and feet, and let them **relax**.	
	Now take a deep breath and let it all out...	
	Think about how heavy your arms and legs can become.	
	Now close your eyes.	
	Breathing induction	
	Focus on your breathing.	

	Become aware of the breath going in and out. Don't force it, don't speed up or slow down. Just breathe naturally and comfortably.	
	When you are ready, on the next breath in, hold it, count silently... slowly... from five down to one... and release the breath.	
	Do this hold-count-release six times, in your own time. While you are doing this you can be curious as to what is happening in your body and notice the changes.	supposition: changes
	[Give the client time to do this]	
	Now... as you let each breath out, say in your mind 'More and more relaxing now'.	
	Keep up the slow, gentle rhythm and as you are thinking 'more and more relaxing now', allow your muscles to relax some more. You can focus on one part of your body or feel it in the whole of your body. Keep on with this process for as long as you want, getting more and more relaxed.	
	Kinesthetic induction	
	Now as you are lying there, breathing gently, relaxing your body...	Pacing
Memory	I wonder if you can remember being inside a tall building somewhere... like a department store... or an office building... a building with a lift [US = elevator] and think about what it feels like to enter that lift...	safety: check in advance your client isn't phobic!
	and in that lift there is a set of buttons... from the tenth floor to the ground floor... and you are going to **press** the button for the ground floor... and you can **feel** the button under your finger... and you **press** the button... all the way in... **sense** the doors shutting... and you **feel** the movement of the lift as it begins to go down...	
	going down and down... and you **feel** yourself gently being **carried** down...	
	and you can become aware as the lift is moving down past each floor... Nine... Eight... and as you **feel the lift passing each floor** you are becoming more and more relaxed... more and more at ease... more and more comfortable... now	Pace with breathing

and Seven... still going down...	
and Six... letting go... **letting it carry** your body down and down...	
and Five... deeper now... more relaxed...	
and Four that lift is still descending and you can **feel it carrying you** down and down...	
Three...	
Two... slowing now	
One... lift almost stopped...	
and you feel the lift come to a stop ... and the doors open.. and you are so relaxed that it is just too much trouble **to move**... so comfortable...	
Kinesthetic deepener	
And it is just like you are lying on a boat or on a swing... and you can feel so comfortable now... feel the gentle movements as you rock from side to side and each movement lets you forget... where you are... who you are... nothing to do... like being on an endless vacation... feeling yourself sinking... down into that soft feeling... and from now on each gentle breath is letting you feel so easy... so comfortable...	
[Continue with the rest of the session]	

Dave Mason © 2010 www.key-hypnosis.com

Breathing Induction

Description: The Breathing induction is a simple and full proof kinesthetic induction.

Method: It works by linking suggestions of relaxation with the natural response everyone has to slowing their breathing. When using this induction watch the person's eyes, if the eyelids start to flicker, you know they are entering trance. For most people this is all the induction you need, but you might want to follow it with a Staircase Deepener if you do not get a clear indication of trance.

Advantages: For most people this is the simplest and most gentle way of getting into trance.

Uses: You can use it on other people or you can use it to put yourself into trance.

Target	Therapist/client	Comment
	Focus on your breathing	
	Are you ready to go into trance?	Yes Set
	I am.	
	Feeling nice and relaxed?	Yes Set
	Yes.	
	Quite comfortable?	Yes Set
	Yes.	
	So, just settle yourself down comfortably. And I'd like you to close your eyes... Thank you.	
Breath 1	OK. What I would like you to do now, [clientname], is just take a deep breath. Take a deep breath... and hold it... That's good.... and now let it go... that's fine... just allow yourself to feel comfortable.	Invoke the para sympathetic relaxation response
Breath 2	Now take another deep breath and hold it. And this time let go all the tension in your shoulders and in your arms... just let that go... that's good.	
Breath 3	And now take another deep breath and hold it... and as you let it go this time just really relax... just allow your body to completely relax... That's very good.	
	Now just resume breathing normally.	Permission Bind
Dissociation	And now I wonder if you could focus on your breathing... just become aware of your	Dissociation Induction

	breathing... how you breathe in and then breathe out... that feeling of your breath in your body... that's excellent...	
	and with each breath out... you might wonder... just exactly how relaxed you could become... with each breath out... think about how your arms and legs can get so heavy... so relaxed... and how comforting that weight can be... and with each breath... your arms and legs... shoulders... muscles... all begin to feel completely relaxed... you become aware of being held safely securely comfortably in that chair... and you are in that chair breathing gently ... listening to my voice... drifting down... and each breath is allowing you to relax more and more... just allowing you to drift away now... that's good...	indirect suggestions
	Countdown Deepener	
	and you might wonder what it would be like to count each breath as you relax... and how each breath can make you more relaxed... and just the thought of breathing and relaxing makes you feel as if you are sinking down... Ten... Nine... going down deeper... Eight... and each breath makes you feel more relaxed... Seven ... and with each breath you feel yourself going deeper and deeper... more and more relaxed... Six... down again.... Five... breathing gently... letting go... Four... down and down... deeper and deeper.... Three... more and more at ease... Two... and One... totally relaxed....	Speak the numbers to match each breath the client makes.

David Mason   www.key-hypnosis.com © 2010

Taste and Smell Hypnosis Induction

Everyone experiences the world differently. Some people are very visual, some pay attention most to what they hear, and some have to touch and feel their world. NLP suggests that no one is totally one or the other, but everyone has a preferred representational style.

A minority of people are mostly experience their world through taste and smell. This is known as the gustatory representational style.

This script focuses most on taste and smell as well as more normal ways to induce trance.

	The visualisation		
	Take a deep breath now... and become aware of all the sensations you are getting in this room right now...		
	Close your eyes... and think about all the sounds and smells you are sensing... think about the feel of your body on the seat... of the weight of your arms and legs...		Dissociation
	Become aware of how...with your eyes closed... relaxing... you could be anywhere...	I	
	and allow your imagination to visualize a lush tropical forest somewhere... trees and vines ... the smell of damp earth and decay hanging in the air... and coloured birds in the trees high above... and down below... deep in the jungle...	V	
	and as you lie there... breathing quietly... relaxing more more with each breath... everything else begins to fade away... each breath making that forest seem more real...	D	
	and in those trees you see an ancient building... like a ruined temple... and there is a doorway... leading in... into a cool quiet place... and you leave all the noise and light and sensations outside...	V	
	and inside is dark and dim... just enough light to see by...		
	and you find yourself going down a long corridor... going deeper and deeper inside that building...	I	Deepener

	and you come to a stone chamber... deep inside... a room set up for some strange purpose... and in that room there is a stone like an altar... it feels as if everything has been set up ... waiting for you... ready to receive you...	
	the room is filled with a smell like incense... a heavy smoky perfume... you find your head dropping... feeling heavy and sleepy... and each breath of that perfume makes you more and more tired...	>
	and there is a seat there ... covered with soft material... and you are so tired it would be so nice to relax now...	D
memory	and as you are relaxing more and more... you notice a small table nearby... and on that table a small box ... and you open the box... and inside are leaves and petals... and a small bottle... with a scent... like the most delicious thing you have ever tasted... and it reminds you of every wonderful thing you have eaten... and you drift away on the memory of that...	V
	and as you breath in more that scent... you feel a wave of relaxation taking you down deeper and deeper...	D
	and on the next gentle breath... that scent takes you even deeper... more and more relaxed... and you find your mind letting go... wandering... wondering... becoming dreamy... and forgetting about those arms and legs...	>
	settling deeper and deeper... at ease now... relaxing more and more with each breath... drifting... down and down... calm and peaceful... warm and comfortable...	
	[either do a deepener, or carry on gently suggesting visualisations involving peace, calm, relaxation]	I

David Mason   www.key-hypnosis.com © 2011

Smoker's Hypnosis induction

A simple effective hypnosis induction Script to Stop Smoking

This hypnosis induction is specially written as the induction to begin a Stop Smoking session. Your whole stop smoking session should be focused on stopping smoking, right from the first words. This induction puts the idea of stopping smoking into the smoker's mind as they go into trance and makes the stop smoking suggestions more effective.

It is a good induction to use because even before your therapy to stop smoking begins you are suggesting clear breath, giving affirmations of 'no more smoking', visualizations of leaving behind the old habit and going to a clean green place as a non smoker.

	Stop Smoking Induction Script		
Capability	Take a deep breath... and let it go... now take another breath... and as you let it go... really relax... and now one more breath as you start the process of becoming a non smoker...	I	Bind
Capability	That's right... and now let your eyes close... and feel that relaxation spreading.	K	Supposition
	And now notice your breathing... now that you have decided to stop smoking... you might senses a difference in your breathing now... or maybe later... you will find you can become aware of your breath as it goes down into your chest... and thinking about how much you can feel of each breath inside... as you breath out... allow your body to relax... more and more...	>	Seeding relaxation
	And as you relax... imagine all that old stuff coming out of your lungs... clearing and healing... relaxing...	V	
	And with each breath out... it is as if there is a voice inside taking over... and you hear the words... *'letting it go... no more smoking'...' letting it go... no more smoking'*... and allow yourself to relax into that rhythm... *' letting it go... no more smoking'*...	A	Reassurance
Behaviour	And I wonder if you can imagine being in a place outside somewhere... and you look around... and everything seems stale and	V	Metaphor

	tired... everything is old and worn out... and the whole atmosphere feels dull and dark and pointless...		
	And you look around... and off to the side... there is an exit... and you decide to take that exit... and behind the exit... there are ten steps going down...		a way out
	and you want to go down those steps... but something seems to be holding you back... and then you realize there is something weighing you down... and you become aware that to go forward...you have to leave something behind... to go down those steps... you need to let go of something... to show it your power...	M	Metaphor
	and you realize that part of you is holding on to an old pack of cigarettes... and there are ten inside...	M	old habits
	and as you step down the top step... you take one of the cigarettes... and you throw it away... and as you go down... you say TEN... and go deeper... and on the next step... you throw away another cigarette... NINE... and relaxing gets easier... and shredding another cigarette... EIGHT... more and more relaxed now... and then SEVEN... another cigarette destroyed... and SIX... going down deeper now... more and more relaxed... FIVE... and FOUR... and THREE... then only two cigarettes away from freedom... TWO... and one to go... throwing away the last ONE...		Countdown induction
	And just drifting away now... feeling clean and clear... and you find yourself in a beautiful place... healthy and clean... green and soft and filled with light...		
	And in that place you know you can relax now because the burden of having to smoke has been lifted off you.. and you can feel yourself changing...	D	
	and some smokers know they are changing because they can feel themselves getting lighter... other smokers feel themselves getting heavier as they are drift away from those old		All possibilities

needs...		

David Mason   www.key-hypnosis.com © 2011

Christian Induction

Many people believe scare stories about hypnosis and its supposed power over people. In particular some churches have been wrongly blamed for demonizing hypnosis. In fact all major churches approve of hypnosis when used in a therapeutic way.

However, the result is that in many people's minds, hypnosis is equated with being anti-Christian. This Christian induction script uses a form of words that are acceptable to Christians, and uses imagery and ideas that Christians will be familiar and comfortable with.

Target	Induction Reassurance		Comments
Behavior	Now you know that hypnosis is a natural state... something that has been given to all people as a way into healing and deep relaxation...		Reassurance
	and when hypnosis is used the way it was intended to be used, it is a form of grace... a blessing for health and recovery... a way of releasing wrong thoughts and feelings... in a safe and healthy way... a way that accords with your deepest principles...		Legitimacy
	Hypnosis is simple and natural... and all you have to do is to breathe... you don't have to do anything else... just breathe and listen to the words... Is that OK with you?		
	[get response]	Y	Yes Set 1
	So are you ready to start with hypnosis?		
	[get response]	Y	Yes Set 2
	I am going to lightly touch you on the forehead. Is that OK?		
	[get response]	Y	Yes Set 3
	Let the Spirit enter		
	So I would like you now to close your eyes.... so lie back and allow your arms and legs to relax as you start to go into hypnosis... at first you won't feel anything different but soon you will start to enjoy the relaxation spreading through your whole body...	I	Breathing induction
	so now take a deep breath... and allow your shoulders to relax... that's good	I	

	and another deep breath... and feel those legs relaxing...	
	and one more breath and allow your eyes to relax... that's right...	
	and now focus on your breathing... become aware of the gentle in and out of your breath...	
	and imagine what it would be like to be filled with the spirit ... and as you breath in... imagine the spirit is entering you... relaxing you... making you more comfortable...	
	and imagine that as you breath out... you are breathing away all tensions... all cares... and letting the spirit fill you...	
	and as the spirit enters... you are relaxing more and more... each breath is relaxing you... as you go deeper and deeper relaxed...	
	and continue breathing in that spirit and feel the difference as it allows you to let go...	
	That's right... continue breathing and relaxing... completely...	
	Countdown Visualization of Guide	
	and I wonder if you can imagine a hillside somewhere... a green hill... far away... and in the distance you can see a silver city... with spires and domes... filled with light...	V
	and a figure appears beside you... a gentle calming figure.. and you feel a deep sense of wisdom... and the figure takes you by the hand and leads you towards a path...	
	and that path leads gently down towards that city... and you go down that path... safe and confident with the figure beside you...	
	and there are ten steps in front of you... and the figure says 'as I lead you down each step, you will feel more comfortable... more relaxed... more at ease'.	Pace with breathing
	and going down each step now... 'and your guide says... Ten... '	
	and Nine... deeper and deeper relaxing...	
	and Eight... more and more relaxed...	
	and Seven... letting go now... allow yourself to	

be led deeper and deeper with each breath...		
and Six...		
and Five... letting go... surrendering to the feeling of being filled with a gentle spirit...		
and Four... the spirit is now moving in you and every part of you is relaxing... letting go... allowing the spirit to take over...		
and Three... feeling yourself sinking down... deeper and deeper		
and Two...		
and One...		
and drifting in that spirit now... surrounded... uplifted... fulfilled...		
Deepener and eye catalepsy test		
Now I am going to gently touch you on the forehead... you will feel a gentle touch... and that will lead you safely into hypnosis... and you might be surprised at how pleasant it feels...		Kinesthetic induction
[draw your finger gently across the forehead horizontally]		
and as you feel that touch you can focus all your attention on that feeling...		
[now draw your finger softly down the middle of the forehead to make the cross]		
and as you feel that symbol being drawn you know you are safe and can relax...		
[keep stroking your finger softly across and down the middle of the forehead]		
and now just focus the whole of your attention on that touch... and as you feel that stroke... you will feel yourself relaxing more and more... and as you feel the touch slowly going down... you feel yourself going down... deeper and deeper... and as you feel that touch going across you feel your mind expanding...		
[now start touching the skin lightly with your finger tip along the lines of the cross, and keep touching here and there very very softly]		
and each touch makes you more aware of how relaxed you can become...		
and feel that relaxation spreading to your		

	forehead... to your eyes...	
	and focus your attention on those eyelids... feel the whole area around your eyes changing... and imagine that those eyes are just unable to open... and allow that feeling to grow...	eye catalepsy
	and as you are relaxing you are allowing the spirit to move within you... to make the spirit manifest...	
	and the spirit can show its presence by making those eyes so tired... so tired and heavy... so heavy that you just can't open them... to feel as if those eyes have forgotten how to work... as if those eyes are glued tight shut...	
	and when the spirit is present you can do the most amazing things... the spirit can relax those eyes all the way down to the point where they just don't work...	
	and when you are sure that the Spirit has closed those eyes all the way down...	
	you can try to open those eyes... and you will experience the power of the spirit... you cannot open those eyes... and the harder you try ... the harder they stay shut...	
	[await response ... and carry on with the therapy]	

David Mason   www.key-hypnosis.com © 2011

Erotic Inductions

Erotic Hypnosis Foreplay Induction

Erotic Hypnosis Induction is a sexual foreplay induction used in erotic seduction. This erotic induction will hypnotize your lover and give her an orgasm she will never forget. Hypnotized women love this induction. It is very sensual, very gentle, very intimate. Hypnotic foreplay increases the erotic pleasure of sex for girls and women. Hypnosis seduction is the ideal sexual foreplay technique and hypnotized women can't get enough of it.

This erotic hypnosis script focuses on touching. This increases sexual response in females if you keep gently, slowly... stroking... murmuring soft words ... suggesting relaxation and sexual feelings... most women become very aroused very quickly.

Women love erotic hypnosis inductions and the gentle stroking sensation of this erotic induction will anchor her female sex response to your words and fingers.

The Erotic Hypnosis induction is a loving way of increasing your partner's erotic response and giving her an orgasm. It is a wonderful form of sexual foreplay. Works for men and women. Try it.

	Erotic induction the set up		*Comments*
Position	You should have your lover lying with her head in your lap, relaxed, somewhere comfortable, with no distractions or sudden noises. She should have only loose clothes on...		
Reach	You should arrange the positions so that you can easily touch her forehead, without any awkward straining, because you will be doing it for quite a while. You might want to use a little skin cream or something from her makeup bag as a lubricant for your fingers. The head can become very heavy after a while so make sure you are both comfortable in your body positions.		
	Erotic hypnotic induction		
	[This section is said to your partner]		
	I would like you to take a deep breath now... and then just let it out...		Breathing Induction
	Now settle yourself comfortably... let your head relax... your neck relax...		
	take another deep breath... and let it out... that's		

	right...	
	and now let your shoulders relax... your arms loose and floppy... let your tummy relax...	Relaxation induction
	one last breath... and let it go...	
	and let your thighs relax... let your legs lie heavy and still... if you are not comfortable arrange yourself so you are completely at ease... and relax deeply...	
	and when you are ready to relax completely... let your eyes close...	Bind
	[Now start gently, *very gently*... start rubbing the forehead in little soft circles ... about the size of a large coin... in the middle of the forehead... you should be barely touching the skin... keep rubbing and circling and gently brushing the skin... occasionally lifting your fingers away briefly... while you talk in a soft voice...]	
	I want you to focus your attention on the feel of my fingers on your skin... become aware of those gentle touches... focus on enjoying that little light touch... feel the brush on the texture of your skin... you can become intensely sensitive to that touch... to the sensation on your skin...	Distraction Induction
	Think about that touch... that sensation... a gentle loving touch... and begin to settle into relaxation to enjoy the sensuous feel of touch on your skin... flesh on flesh...	K
	[keep gently stroking and touching the forehead all the while... very slowly, very soft...]	
memory	I wonder if you can remember lying somewhere completely relaxed... somewhere warm and comfortable... somewhere you feel safe and at ease...	Safe place
	and as you feel each little stroke on your skin, you can allow yourself to relax more... think about the touch on your skin, and how that can make you feel more at ease... more comfortable...	
	[keep gently stroking and touching... very slowly, very softly... now start moving a little wider on the skin... start touching with the tip of one finger only... touching down... lifting off...	

	touching down... lifting off...getting wider and wider across the forehead...]	
	And as you think about that touching... you can feel your body... the position of your arms and legs... feel the weight of them... heavy and relaxed...	
	and with each touch you can feel yourself sinking... releasing... letting go...	
	with each touch you can feel the tension leaving your body... your shoulders relax... your chest relaxing... your tummy relaxing now... and your thighs... soft and open and easing with each gentle touch...	
	[keep gently touching with the tip of one finger only... touching down... lifting off... touching down... lifting off... now start stroking down on each side of the brow... stroking the eyebrows... barely touching]	
	And as you feel each touch going down... you feel yourself going down... you mind drifting deeper and deeper... relaxed...	Pace voice with each stroke
	that's right... that's good... that's your body responding the way it should... =	Reassurance
	and as you feel that touch on your skin... you begin to feel a warmth spreading through your body... a tingling... alive feeling... as your body relaxes even more... you can become aware of sensual feeling stirring... rising... as I touch each part... it is like a tingle there... arousing... opening ... freeing you to enjoy being female...	
	[now carry on touching further down, touching the lips, etc. Develop the script by suggesting that each touch on the skin causes a feeling in an intimate part of the body, that every stroke can be felt like a tingle of electricity... etc.]	

David Mason   www.key-hypnosis.com © 2011

Erotic Hypnosis Head Massage sex induction

This is a lovely way to relax your partner and get ready for sex. Massaging the face and head is sensual and intimate and this script shows how to do it properly and how to combine it with an erotic hypnosis induction.

This process has to be done very gently. The neck is very delicate - No sudden movements, no excess force, no twisting or pushing. Everything should be a caress, sliding your hands over her scalp and skin, soft and loving, slow and gentle.

A gentle massage before sex

	Set up	
	Position your partner so that she is sitting comfortably in a way that you can stand behind her and you are able to move to the side of her. If she has long hair tied up then get her to let it down. Ask her to take her glasses off and you remove your watch.	
	Standing behind her say...	
	Now I want you to be sitting comfortably... try just moving your head around... loosen up your neck muscles... lift up your shoulders and let them drop... waggle your arms around and then lay them in your lap...	Relax muscles of her neck and shoulders
	I am going to give you a lovely neck and head massage... Is that OK?	Get permission
	Now if at any time you feel I am pressing too hard, or you feel uncomfortable in any way... just say so, OK?	Safety
	The shoulder massage	
	stand behind her and place your hands lightly on her shoulders...	
	Now I would like you to take three deep breaths... and as you breath out... really let yourself relax...	D
	1. Now start gently squeezing the muscle that runs along the top of the shoulder up to the neck. First, squeeze the muscle close to her neck with each	

	hand, then move and squeeze in the middle... and then squeeze again near the shoulder. Do this very softly to start with.	
	And as you feel my hands gently moving on your body... you can begin to pay attention to your breathing	I	Start breathing induction
	2. Then repeat the three squeezes again... a little more firmly...	
	and as you breath in and out... you can feel your body starting to relax	D
	3. Then repeat the three squeezes on more time... a little more firmly still...	
	Relaxing more and more... feel those muscles loosening... softening... relaxing..	D	pace and lead
massage the spine		
	1. Now move your hands close to her neck, still resting on her shoulders... and place your thumbs on each side of the spine... just below her collarbone	
	begin to make small circles close to spine on each side...	
	and now feel that tension easing out of you neck...	D
	then move your fingers up above the collar bone... and continue to make small circles with your thumbs on each side...	
	enjoy that feeling as those muscles ease and relax and let go...	D
	continue to move your fingers up the back of her neck... in little steps... until you reach her hairline...	
	feel that relaxation spreading to other parts of your body...	D	Ambiguity
	2. now go back to below the collarbone again... and repeat the little circles , applying just a little more pressure each time.	
	just relax and enjoy that feeling	
	3.and repeat the little circles again, applying just a little more thumb pressure	
	that's right... feel the tension going...	D	Presupposition
arm roll		

1. put your forearms on her shoulders near the neck with your thumbs pointing up. Now roll your arms across her shoulders until your palms are facing up.		
rolling away all the tension	D	
2. lift your forearms to a position near the middle with your thumbs pointing up. Now roll your arms again.		
letting your shoulders relax	D	
3. put your forearms on her shoulders near her arms and roll your arms again.		
really relaxing now...	D	
repeat the arm roll process two more times.		
even more relaxing now... and as you feel that rolling pressure... imagine the relaxation going all down your body...	>	
neck massage		
Move to her left side and put your left hand on her forehead, and your right hand at the base of her neck.		
And now I am going to move to the side and touch you on your forehead. Feel the warmth of my hand on your skin. Feel that warmth spreading through your mind and down into your body...		
1.using just the thumb and index finger, slide your hand gently up the sides of her neck. When you reach the hair line, squeeze very gently, and hold it there..		
Feel the gentle touch of my hand on the back of your neck... enjoy that feeling of pressure where my fingers touch your skin... allow that feeling to reach deep inside and release...		
2.slide your hand gently up the sides of her neck again and when you reach the hair line, squeeze gently and hold.		
feel the pleasure of that pressure spreading down your back... down your hips... all the way down...		
3. repeat the procedure as often as you want, squeezing gently at the hairline each time, and circling on the upstroke if you like.		
And as those fingers slide up your neck... you can		

	feel a tingling relaxation spreading though your body...	
	and each gentle circle is loosening your muscles... loosening your chest... your tummy... your hips... your hands...	
Head rock		
	Now keeping your left hand on her forehead, move your right hand to the top of her neck..	
	Gently (GENTLY!) slowly rock her head forward, so her forehead goes down, without straining or excessive movement, and then move it backwards till her face is looking up. Very, very gently.	SAFETY!
	And as that head goes down... you feel yourself letting go ... letting go to enjoy the pleasure of rocking and moving and swaying... safe and secure...	
	and as that head moves back and forward... you can allow your mind to drift away... to some pleasant place... like rocking a child...	
	safe and warm and comfortable...	
Scalp massage		
	Now step behind her. Put your hands on each side of her head with the fingers spread apart. Allow her head to tip back a little and support it if you need to.	
	1. Slowly move your hands towards the top of her head with a shampooing motion.	
Memory	and as you feel each movement of the hands this reminds you of how relaxed you can become	
	2. Move your hands to another part of her head and repeat the shampooing motion.	
Memory	the feeling reminds you of warm baths... relaxing by a pool perhaps... outdoors of the grass... remember what it feels like to really let go...	
	3. Keep moving your hands to other parts of her head and repeat the shampooing motion until you have gently massaged the whole surface of her head.	
	Really relaxing... nothing to think about... nothing to do... just surrender to the lovely feeling of fingers stroking and caressing your skin	

Scalp running		
Form your hands into a claw shape. You are going to use both hands to run your fingers down her scalp starting at the hairline on her brow all the way down to the hairline at the back of her neck.		
1. Start with both hands together and comb down the center line of her head.		
and as you feel those fingers running down your scalp you feel sensations deep inside your body...		
2. Move your hands apart and start from the front hair line again.		
sensations of warmth and openness... of longing and needing... feelings going deep inside and lighting up desires..		
3. Move your hands apart again and run your fingers along her scalp just above the ears and down to her neck. Repeat as often as you want.		
And each stroke you feel is stroking your desire... your need to be touched and caressed... to have your whole body rubbed and aroused...		
Finger combing		
Now pull her head back so it is resting on your stomach. You are going to comb your fingers through her hair, over and over, suggesting all the time that she is feeling more and more aroused with each stroke.		
1. put the fingers of both hands on her forehead. Slowly move them up across her skin and then pull them back through her hair as if you are combing her hair with you fingers.		
And now enjoy that lovely feeling of being caressed... as each stroke slides through your hair you can feel those passions rising inside you..		
you feel the warmth of my body against the back of your head...		
you feel the beat of my heart as we breath together...		
2. Gradually move them out to the side of her forehead. Then up across her skin and then pull them back through her hair as if you were stroking a purring cat.		

allow yourself to feel every warm feeling you ever had... coming out now... enjoying that feeling of release as you feel your hair being stroked...	
3. Now move them out to the side of her head, and begin making soft circular motions on her temples, the dimples just above a line between the corner of her eyes and top of her ears.	
Each each motion, each touch is making you...	
[go on to make whatever erotic suggestions you prefer]	

David Mason   www.key-hypnosis.com © 2011

Erotic Foreplay Sexy Oil Massage

Erotic Foreplay Sex Massage to increase women's sensuality and get ready for sex. This Foreplay Sex Massage script shows you exactly what to do to take her to orgasm. It incorporates all the senses. Erotic Foreplay Sex Massage uses your voice, your hands, and the senses of smell, touch and taste and imagination to create a sensuous sexy foreplay game. You can use erotic oil massage to give her a full orgasm, or as the first stage for longer sexual play.

Hypnosis Sex is gentle and consensual and this lets you combine stroking and caressing with hypnotic suggestion until she is almost at orgasm.

What you do after that is up to you. Expect to get invited back. Soon.

The Setup		
Success in sensual sex depends on preparation.		
Make sure the room is warm and free from drafts.		
Make sure you won't be disturbed - turn off the phone, alarms, the TV, anything that is likely to distract you and break the erotic hypnotic spell.		
You can use very soft instrumental music for background.		
Turn the lights down, or use candles to set the mood. Make sure there are no lights shining in her eyes.		
If you have them, use scented candles to create a sensuous atmosphere.		
Get some baby oil or scented massage oil. If you don't have oil you can use moisturizing cream, but it is not as easy to apply. Do not use the scented oils designed for burning in lamps.		
Make sure the oil is at body heat. You can stand it in some warm water before you start, or you can warm it against your body for a few minutes.		
Best to have her lying on a bed or a sofa or couch where she can stretch out.		
Have her stretch out naked lying on her back on an old sheet or some towels. The massage oil always		

spills, so do not use the regular bed coverings, and use something to protect furnishing fabrics as they can get stained with oil.		
Hypnotic Induction		
Are you comfortable there?		Safety
[get agreement]		
Are you ready for a sensual adventure?		check
Ok. Now close your eyes and take a deep breath. That's good.		eyes closed
Now take another deep breath and really relax. Let it all go. Leave everything else to me.		beginning of induction
The fantasy massage induction		
And now I wonder if you can imagine a warm day somewhere. You are on vacation. You are lying in the sun. Imagine lying in the sun relaxing... on a boat... far out at sea... nothing around for miles... you are lying there sunbathing naked... like a film star on a yacht... you are pleasantly relaxed... comfortable...		
and as you feel the sun gently warming your body... you are relaxing even more... like lying on a soft fleecy cloud... with a little gentle rocking motion ... making you even more relaxed...		
and as you imagine yourself on that boat... a boat drifting away... floating... gliding...	V	
[start dripping a few drops of oil on her belly]		
you become aware of someone kneeling beside you... and a few drops of oil slowly spreading on your skin... and a hand stroking and caressing you		focus of attention
[start rubbing the oil on her stomach in long slow circles.]		
and as that hand starts to circle slowly you are getting more relaxed... dreaming of being on that boat... warm and comfortable...	K	
and focusing on that slow soft movement makes you feel detached... and all of your attention is drawn to following the movement of that hand... as it glides slowly softly across your skin...		focus of attention
and as that hand circles round and round you can feel yourself slowly letting go... just enjoying the sensation... nothing to think about... only the soft warm feel of that hand... smooth and gentle...	>	movement = relaxation

and each stroke of the hand is leading your mind away... relaxing deeper and deeper now...	D
[now start rubbing one finger or thumb down her tummy, then lift it and start again at the top, over and over.]	
and as you relax more... each stroke is taking you down and down... feeling that movement makes you more detached...	
and every sound you hear will take you deeper and deeper...	audio deepener
and every touch on your skin now takes you deeper and deeper...	kinesthetic deepener
and every breath now is taking you deeper and deeper...	breathing deepener
more relaxed... that's right... letting go... that's the way it's supposed to be...	Reassurance
Sensual Massage Section	
[drip more oil on between her breasts. Start massaging in tiny circular movements]	
and now focus on the movements on your chest. Become aware of those movements... and as you become aware of those movements... you can become aware of something else... a feeling stirring deep inside you...	
[now start making the circles bigger, going over the rise of her breasts.]	
and feeling that movement on your breasts... becoming aware of a feeling starting in your breasts... and each touch passes... that feeling grows stronger and stronger...	
[start rubbing the oil around her breasts, softly rising up towards, but never touching, the nipples.]	
and you are becoming more and more aware of that feeling now... your breasts are beginning to fill... you are enjoying that sensuous feeling... growing more and more with each touch...	
[start circling around the aureole, with a very delicate touch, avoiding actually touching her nipples, but very close in long slow circles.]	
now you can feel the heat there... filling and rising and aching for more...	

[now put more oil on her tummy, and begin to rub around it with the flat of your hand... more long slow circles.]		
and now that feeling is moving down... down to where the hand is rubbing... circling... feel that warmth and passion rising up...	>	
and as the hand moves round each movement lets you feel more intense... more and more feelings coming up now... and as that hand moves down your body... down to that special area... you feel your body getting more aroused... more sensuous... more alive... you feel yourself getting warm and wet... and every movement of that hand is making you more sensitive... to the feeling on your skin... to the feeling in your body...	D	
[start rubbing around her genital area... not on it... around it.]		
and now you are becoming aware of a need... a compulsion... a wanting... a desire...	D	
[start rubbing the oil on her thighs... drawing your oily fingers up her legs in long slow strokes.]		
and as each strokes rises up your thighs... you feel that passion rising in you... making you soft and wet and open and ready...		
ready to climax... ready to give and receive... all your feelings now concentrated in that one special private area... and each stroke on your thighs is making you feel special... ready... wanting... to open to receive and thrust and every movement every sound every feeling is making you more aware of your needs... to be touched to be caressed to be filled...		
and all that feminine power is opening up now... you feel your body ready to quiver to throb and move and thrust as the feeling gets stronger and stronger...		
Reorientation section		
[continue stroking and suggesting for as long she can take it... or lean your body over hers and kiss her deeply... and just see what happens... enjoy.]		
When you are both done, wrap yourselves in the sheet or towels. Lie close beside her with your arms around her, you head against hers and hold her for as long as		

	she wants.			

David Mason   www.key-hypnosis.com © 2011

Hypnosis Seduction Sex Game

This hypnosis sex seduction game is a light-hearted way to start having fun with women. The seduction sex game is easy to learn and easy impress her with your hypnotic powers.

Just introduce your hypnotic seduction routine as a fun party game. Talk to a bunch of girls and ask them they believe in hypnosis, and if one of them would be interested in doing an experiment in mind control.

You can play the sex game with several girls at the same time if you want to. That can let you get a girl to feel more at ease.

During the hypnosis sex game most women will go into trance immediately, and then want to talk about it, and you will get a reputation as a pick up artist. Even the girls who don't go into trance will still have experienced sexual feelings whether she admits or not, and that will give you an opening to talk about other seks games.

	Seduction sex game Set up		comments
	The woman should be standing in front of you. You need to get her permission to touch her. Ask her is she up for a seduction game or tell her it is a fun game to get a girl to relax and enjoy a new experience.		
	Erotic hypnotic Sex game induction		
	[This section is said to your volunteer]		
	I am going to ask you to join me in an experiment in mind control,		sets up expectation
	to see how good an imagination you have.		bind
	I wonder if you are the type of woman who feels connections between her imagination and her feelings?...		will want to prove this too
	If she say 'Yes' say 'that's right, that's one of things people like about you'. If she says 'No' say 'Well let's see, shall we? I think you might be surprised'.		deal with both possibilities
	Hold your hands out in front of you, elbows bent, arms close to the body,with the palms facing upwards.		
	In a moment I going to touch the palms of your hands... is that OK?		
	[Get permission] [Move her hands into the right position if you have to.]		get permission
	Now I want you to close your eyes and take a		

	deep breath... and let it go...	
	Now focus all your attention on the palms of your hands... become aware of all the feelings you have in the palms of your hands...	
	[Begin to make very light circling movements on her palms].	
	Now imagine those gentle strokes are reminding you of a time when you felt sensual and feminine and lovable... allow those soft touches to bring to mind caressing and stroking and all the feelings that brings up for you...	
	Don't try to analyses it or think about it... just feel the feeling... imagine that feeling is there... swirling around on the palms of your hands...	
	[keep making light circling movements on her palms].	Hypnotic induction
	and each gentle touch is making you focus more and more on your hands...	D
	and that feeling is getting stronger and stronger...	D
memory	reminding you of the best feeling you ever had...	I
	and with each breath out... you feel your body relaxing...	D
	and just focusing on that feeling swirling round on your hands... getting stronger... deeper...	D
	and each breath is making you focus more and more on that wonderful feeling... that's right...	Pace with signs of trance
	and you feel it building up... sensations of warmth... tingling... brightness... looseness... color... energy...	
	And if that energy was a color... what color would it be?	Test for dissociation
	[get a response eg Purple].	
	That's right... and now imagine that Purple energy getting brighter and stronger and bigger than before...	Pace voice with each stroke
	[start stroking her fingers and wrists while you talk].	= Reassurance
	and as that purple energy builds up... as you feel those touches on your skin... that feeling intensifies... and you feel yourself letting go...	

enjoy that feeling...	
[now move your fingers underneath her hands... and stroke from the back of her wrists along her fingers while you talk. Keep doing this until her hands start to move.]	
and that strange feeling in your hands is making you think of other feelings... and those hands are now starting to move upwards... towards your body... and as they do... that swirling feeling is getting stronger...	
and allow those hands to drift up... carrying those feelings... that purple energy... that warmth... that tingle is getting carried up now... and those hands are moving towards your body...	Pace with the movements of her hands
[her hands will come up against her breasts...].	
and feel that energy being transferred from those hands to your body... feel your body responding... taking in that energy... filling... responding... let those hands start to spread that energy around as you move those those hands stroking and caressing...	
and that energy begins to spread through your body... waking other feelings... creating tingling... swelling... enjoying... and those hands can spread that feeling all over...	
and want to reach out to someone... to stroke and caress and explore... to spread that feeling even more...	
[now carry on with further sex games and playful ways to get a girl interested.]	

David Mason   www.key-hypnosis.com © 2011

Stealth Inductions

Conversational Induction

This style of hypnosis is called conversational hypnosis, or covert hypnosis, and is normally used to avoid resistance in clients who will not accept formal hypnosis. It is seldom used in therapy because standard methods are faster and easier. However it is promoted aggressively on the Internet by people claiming to be able to reveal the secret of 'covert hypnosis' and 'how to get other people to do whatever you want' or to 'secretly hypnotize women'. In fact, there is nothing mysterious or secret about the process of analogical marking. Anyone can learn it. All it needs is a bit of planning and a bit of practice.

In order for a command to go unnoticed in a normal conversation the command must be short, and not stand out as something strange or odd in the normal speech it is embedded in. It needs to be subtle and not overused. The commands can be mixed in with any topic at all, although the hypnotist would usually choose a topic that the client was familiar with, but choose to talk about it in a slightly ambiguous or unusual way, so as to engage the client's attention.

Basic Procedure for analogical marking

The first thing to do is decide what words and phrases you want to put into the other person's mind using analogical marking.

Then write these out in the order that you want to deliver them.

Then select a topic that will engage the client's interest.

Create a narrative using the topic. The story should be intriguing, ambiguous and little 'off beat' in order to get the client thinking and wondering where it might be going, or the analogical marking might stick out. The script can go off into sub stories (see Multiple Embedded Metaphor Therapy) and use any of the hypnotic wording techniques that are part of normal hypnotic induction language. Analogical marking does not need to be grammatical, logical or even complete, because the client will be in trance by the time the story is part way through.

The script below shows how analogical marking commands can be embedded into anything. In this case the story is an unlikely and unpromising topic just to demonstrate how it can be done. The text can be read in two ways. The first version shows the text as delivered: there is nothing to signal that it is actually aimed at inducing trance. Reading the second version shows that the embedded commands for analogical marking make up a complete induction, and the words surrounding them are just to distract the mind.

Without analogical marking

I wonder if you have ever thought about motor racing and therapy? You know what a race track is like... high tech cars whizzing round a race track at great speed might not seem to have a lot to do with how to... make yourself relax, ... but great racing drivers have an amazing ability, even in all that noise and speed they can... get comfortable... in any situation. Good drivers have learned to... let go of any tension ...before the race, they prepare themselves mentally... so that they are ready before it all begins... and then during the race they can get so focused they... forget about everything else ... around them, they climb into the car... buckle the harness... and then they visualize how it will be... going round that track... in their mind... then they allow the mind to empty... become one with the car and the surroundings... not noticing... focusing internally... becoming aware of the feeling under their fingertips... head back and eyes closed for a moment... focusing on each breath out...they settle down... becoming aware of their body's weight... arms and legs...

sinking down into that comfortable seat, and as it gets going, things seem to happen in slow motion, as if everything has slowed down completely... it seems as if they are just drifting slowly round the corners, then down the straights, and as they sit there, in control of things... in control of the car...so relaxed and focused, and then down... further down through the gears, smoothly and steadily... and then comfortably into the straight, relaxed and breathing gently ... part of the driver's mind considers what it has to consider, and another part thinks about forgetting things it doesn't have to ... and they say the best way is to just let go... let go of all thoughts, to really enjoy the feeling... of being in control, of going inward, focus on that feeling of inner calm that comes when... nothing matters... there is nothing to do... all the preparation is done... running smoothly down... on track towards the reward... everything is going the way it is supposed to... and as the minutes pass gently away... and the race winds down... and things get slower and slower as the cars reach the finish... totally at rest...

With analogical marking

I wonder if you have ever thought about motor racing and therapy? You know what a race track is like...high tech cars whizzing round a race track at great speed might not seem to have a lot to do with how to...

make yourself relax, ...but great racing drivers have an amazing ability, even in all that noise and speed they can... **get comfortable**... in any situation. Good drivers have learned to... **let go of any tension** ...before the race, they prepare themselves mentally... so that they are ready before it all begins... and then during the race they can get so focused they...

forget about everything else ... around them, they climb into the car... buckle the harness... and then they visualize how it will be... going round that track... in their mind... then they **allow the mind to empty...** become one with the car and the surroundings... not noticing... focusing internally... becoming aware of the feeling under their fingertips... head back and eyes closed for a moment... **focusing on each breath out**...they settle down... becoming aware of their body's weight... arms and legs...

sinking down into a comfortable seat, and as it gets going, things seem to happen in slow motion, as if everything has slowed down completely... it seems as if they are **just drifting slowly** round the corners, then down the straights, and as they sit there, in control of things... in control of the car...so **relaxed** and focused, and then **down...**

further down through the gears, smoothly and steadily... and then **comfortably** into the straight, **relaxed** and **breathing gently** ... part of the driver's mind considers what it has to consider, and another part thinks about forgetting things it doesn't have to ... and they say the best way is to **just let go... let go of all thoughts,** to really enjoy the feeling...

of being in control, of going inward, focus on that feeling of inner calm that comes when... **nothing matters**... there is **nothing to do**... all the preparation is done... running **smoothly down**... on track towards the reward... everything is going the way it is supposed to... and as the minutes **pass gently away**... and the race winds **down**... and things get slower and slower as the cars reach the finish ... **totally at rest**...

How to mark embedded commands

The embedded commands to use with analogical marking can be marked in various ways. There is no right or wrong way to do a conversational induction, as long as the analogical marking is consistent and non-obvious

Voice tone

Voice tone is the most useful way of marking out specific words. Humans recognise that the tone of voice implies something over and above the actual words used. Saying a word with a descending, deepening tone of voice turns it into a command, or at least something you should be paying attention to. On the other hand, saying a word with the voice rising at the end turns it into a question.

When talking to a client to perform a conversational induction, the hypnotist can speak the command words more loudly, or with a particular stress, or in a different accent, or by turning their head either towards or away from the client. All of these forms of analogical marking are easy to do and many people already do it naturally and unconsciously. Politicians are trained to 'lean forward and smile' while delivering their core message to the interviewer.

Caution

Analogical marking has to be done with some care. If it is done in a clumsy way then the listener will realise that they are being manipulated. They will immediately reject what the speaker says from then on. After that, any kind of trust has been lost forever.

Similarly, as with all unconscious suggestions, the unconscious mind will not do anything that is against that person's moral or ethical codes. In sales, cleverly done analogical marking can be used to plant ideas such as 'good value' or 'decide today' or similar because these are part of the normal buying and selling process. However, no matter how a suggestion is delivered, you cannot get anyone to do things that they would not ordinarily do. Any suggestion or command, even if it has been introduced subtly and progressively, will be rejected if it clashes with that person's inner values.

NLP Anchoring Hypnosis Script

This script is partly an induction and partly hypnotherapy. As the client thinks about their issue, they are actually going into trance, which is why this script is included with the inductions.

NLP Anchoring creates a link between an internal feeling and an external event such as a touch or a sound. The following script shows how to use anchoring in therapy. The hypnotic logic of the script is shown below. This anchoring script uses two positive anchors, one based on competence and one based on anger. These are anchored by causing pain in the tender skin around the thumbnail. Then the anchoring script brings up the negative emotions. Finally the anchor is fired to swamp the painful feelings with positive and powerful emotions.

This NLP Anchoring script is powerful way of eliminating old hurts and fears. The anchoring script uses standard NLP techniques and also incorporates visualisation techniques and symbolism.

Structure of the script

Recall a positive state

> Ask the person to recall a time when they felt 'in control', or 'powerful' or 'in charge'. Get them to really get into the feeling that they felt at that time, to not just think about it, but to experience it, to 'be there'.

Intensify the positive state

> Then ask them to intensify that feeling, to double it and double it again. Get them to become immersed in the emotion, in the feeling. When they are right in that emotional state you should be able to see physical changes, in their face, or how they hold themselves or in changed breathing patterns.

Anchor the positive state

> When they are in the positive state, create the anchor. Familiar things like a clenched fist already have associations so it is better to create a unique anchor. This anchoring script uses pressing a fingernail against the thin skin at the top of the thumbnail to create the link.

Recall the negative state

> Then get the person to go into the bad feelings they want to get rid of. This NLP anchoring script allows the person to safely be in that negative experience, to feel it as something outside of them, assures them that they can deal with it.

Mix the positive and negative states

> Then while the person is experiencing the bad feelings - fire the anchor. This will cause the feelings of power and competence to get

mixed up with the bad feelings. The result is that the bad feeling is experienced differently and thus loses its power to hurt.

Target	Relaxing the body...	Comment
	Take a deep breath... and let it go... just relax...	
	Loosen your shoulders... lift your arms and drop them... raise your legs slightly and relax them... just get all the tension out of your muscles...	
	Take another breath... and let it go... and really relax...	
	One more breath... this time as you breath out...Slowly close your eyes...	
	Now breathe normally for a few moments... think about how your arms and legs feel... become aware of the weight of your body...	Give them time to settle down
	Set the first anchor... POWER	
	Now slowly open your eyes and then close them as you breathe out... and allow your body to relax even more...	Fractionation
	Now think back in your life... think back to a time when you had a success... think back to time when you had control... when you felt good about something you had done.. something you achieved... remember that time... allow all of it to come to mind now... remember how you felt... what you saw... what you heard... immerse yourself now in that experience... build it up in your mind until it is like you are there... back in that moment...	Anchor to a time when they felt strong and in charge
	feel it in your body... what it felt like to be there... to be a winner... a success...	Get the feeling
	Bring to mind some object... some symbol... some thing that you associate with that time and that feeling...	Get an image
	And now focus on that symbol... and feel the feeling... and make that feeling stronger and stronger... that feeling of success of triumph of winning... whatever it was	Intensify the feeling
	Now as that feeling grows stronger... as that	Set the anchor

	symbol gets clearer... feel the power in you... and as it builds... PRESS the LEFT THUMB and INDEX FINGER TOGETHER... press the index finger into the tender flesh at the side of the thumbnail or the top of the thumbnail... dig the nail in if you can... get a painful feeling...	
	let the power grow... and as it does press those fingers tighter and tighter...	
	and then release that hand... and let all the tension go... and just relax... the whole of your body	Anchor set
Set the second anchor... ANGER		
	Now slowly open your eyes and then close them again as you breathe out... and allow your body to relax even more...	Fractionation
	Now allow your mind to drift away... think back to some time... some event... some incident... when you felt anger... real anger at something... when you totally refused to go along with something... to let something happen...	
	and imagine now that you are there now... really feel what it is like to be there... back in that situation... take a few moments and experience again how it was to be that angry... that fired up...	Get the feeling
	Now find some thing... some object... some symbol that you associate with that incident... that feeling... something that reminds you of how it is to be that angry... that justified anger...	Get an image
	and as you experience that feeling in your mind... make that symbol that object... stronger and clearer... and make the link between the symbol and the feeling of anger as strong as it can be... in what ever way makes sense to you..	Intensify the feeling
	and when you have the link between that symbol and that feeling really strong... think of the symbol and PRESS the RIGHT FIRST FINGER into the thumbnail skin...	Set the anchor

	feel the fingers digging into each other as you intensify the memory of that anger and the thing that symbolizes it...	
	and then release that hand... and let all the tension go... and just relax... the whole of your body	Anchor set
Bring the unwanted feeling to mind...		
	Now keeping the awareness of both hands in mind... and the strong feelings associated with pressing those fingers tightly together...	Don't lose the anchors!
	slowly open your eyes and then close them again as you breathe out... and allow your body to relax even more...	Franctionation
	Now bring to mind something that symbolises that unwanted feeling you get...	the bad feeling
	become aware of the feeling... let it build up in your mind... feel it in your body...	
Capability	You can do this... you can allow that feeling to come in to your mind... your body... because it is only a memory... and nothing in your own memories can ever harm you...	Reframing = harmless
	and think about what might symbolise that feeling... bring that symbol to mind.. and allow the feeling to come forward...	Set the symbol
	just be curious about the feeling... how you have it... where you feel it... it cannot harm you... you can regard it as if it was something that has come into you... as if you are looking at it sensing it from the outside... a strange thing that has nothing to do with you...	Set the feeling
Fire the anchors...		
	And when you are ready... when you have decided that you have had enough of the feeling... think of the image of that feeling...	Say this fast...
	and then... PRESS BOTH INDEX FINGERS HARD into the thumbs at at the same time... bring to mind those feelings of power and achievement and anger and the symbols of both hands	.. with rising excitement
	let those feelings overwhelm the bad feeling... and those symbols of power combine with and	say it with certainty

	wipe out the symbol of the bad feeling...	
	Feel that power flush through you... see that old feeling being destroyed... feel it twist and die... enjoy the feeling of wiping it out...	
	Test the anchors...	
	Now slowly open your eyes...	
	And try to think of that old situation again... feel what you get now... be aware of how it has changed...	supposition
	[It is sometimes necessary to set and fire the anchors several times to clear everything]	

David Mason   www.key-hypnosis.com © 2010

Hypnotic Depth Test Induction

People vary in how easily they will go into trance. Everyone can be hypnotised, it's just that some are easier than others, and some need more time or a particular approach. It is possible to determine how susceptible each person is, and the Finger Steeple is probably the easiest way to find out. The Finger Steeple is quick and easy to do, and teaches the client that going into trance is in no way mysterious or frightening - hypnosis can happen with the eyes open and fully aware of what is going on. In fact, you don't have to mention hypnosis at all. It immediately convinces people that they personally can be hypnotised and removes any reluctance before it even arises. It can be a fun thing to do in a bar or at a party.

You need to communicate total certainty about what is going to happen to the other person in a subtle but unmistakable way.

The text in green is what puts the idea of a different 'mind space' into the other person's head. Talking about those fingers or that gap in a tone of wonder causes the other person to think of them as being something outside themself and that whatever is happening must be happening because of something outside their control

The text in blue marks the direct suggestion phrases that make the routine work. These must be said with absolute belief in your voice. Unless you totally believe it, the other person won't.

Target	mm:ss	Dialogue	L	Vector
		FINGER STEEPLE Susceptibility Test		
	00:00	What I would like you to do now is to put your hands like that [*demonstrates palms together, hands upright*] ... now like that [*demonstrates clasping*] ... now put your fingers up like so [*demonstrates raising the two index fingers*] with a gap between them, about an inch...		A little bit of theatre to intrigue the person.
	00:28	Now just look at that gap in the middle,		Dissociation

		pay attention to that gap... just allow your mind to relax... and just look at that gap... and as you look at that gap you see those fingers are moving together ... closer and closer...		(narrow the attention)
		that gap is reducing and those fingers are moving ... and it is completely automatic.... and those fingers are now moving closer.... And now those fingers are touching...	D	Direct Suggestion
	00:40	And those fingers are getting tighter and tighter and those fingers are pressing together more and more and more ... and those fingers are stuck together as if they are glued. And you are totally unable to get those fingers apart... you can try moving those fingers but the harder you try the more they stick together... and those fingers are totally stuck.	D	Pile on the suggestions with increased excitement in your voice
	01:00	They are stuck like glue...you can't get them apart... you can try to get them apart but they will not come apart those fingers are totally jammed... and those fingers will be totally jammed until I snap my fingers and say ... ONE TWO THREE [SNAP].	D	Sensory distortion, muscle catalepsy
	01:10	Let them go...		
Capability	01:25	Now that was a demonstration of the power of your mind... your mind is very, very strong ... and you can go into hypnosis very very quickly and easily...	D	Post Hypnotic Suggestion.

The Finger Steeple is actually a test of resistance, not susceptibility.

Everyone should respond to it, so it if doesn't work it means that the person you are testing is actively resisting your suggestions. This tells the hypnotist that an indirect method will need to be used, or that some time will need to be spent finding out why the person is resisting and to overcome their fears. The resistance usually occurs because during the routine the person sees their fingers moving mysteriously and feels that they are losing control, so they will deliberately pull back the fingers.

The routine works on everyone because of human physiology. If you hold your index finger straight up the ligaments in your hand will naturally contract and pull the finger forward. So if you hold both index fingers up they will automatically pull forward, which looks like they are being attracted to each other.

The combination of inevitable physical movement linked to suggestion is very powerful. Most people will report being unable to move their fingers, and at that moment they really believe they can't. In some people you will see their eyes glaze and get a 'spacey' look. For these people all you have to do is say *'In a moment I will count from Three down to One, and when I reach One your hands will drop into your lap and you will fall into a deep trance. Counting now, Three, Two, One. Sleep!'*

Even those people it doesn't work on will be impressed because they will always admit that they saw their fingers beginning to move before they started resisting. Build on this to point out that they were actually going into trance and only their own deliberate intervention prevented it. This usually leads on to a discussion of beliefs about hypnosis and a willingness to try another method.

Re-orienting from trance

Reorientation is the process of bringing the client out of trance. There are many ways to do it, and many ways of doing it wrong. The standard method of telling the client that they will feel wonderful when they open their eyes is generally a bad idea.

I no longer use the '*wow you are feeling fabulous and bursting with energy and everything is bright and wonderful*' type of re-orientation - too many people just do not feel that way when they come out of trance. Given that most of the people who attend hypnotherapy are unhappy in the first place it is to be expected that they don't naturally feel full of fizz just because somebody suggested it.

I find that the majority of people coming out of trance are filled with the wonder of the experience, and what they want is a few moments of quiet to enjoy that amazing feeling. Telling people that they will feel energised and jumping for joy when they were deep in trance a moment ago just does not work. The human body cannot instantly flip from profound relaxation to hyperactivity. Telling people they should feel ecstatic risks disappointing the client. If they don't get the promised feeling they immediately think they have failed. Or worse, they think you have failed, and therefore the session has failed. Better to avoid it.

I find that if there is enough time left in the session it is best to say to the client something like 'And now you can come back to the present in your own time and in your own way'.

There is a belief among some experienced hypnotists, especially stage hypnotists, that the count up re-orientation is a waste of time, and they simply say '*Open your eyes, your mind is clear and you are ready for the rest of your day. Now.*' It seems to work just as well as any other one.

Count out reorientation

This is the standard count out reorientation routine. It gives the client time to go from trance to full alertness, but does not take more than a few seconds. The therapist should pace their words to whatever the client is doing. So if the client starts moving their feet a little, then say '*... and feet moving, legs flexing...*'

	Back to the present...		
	In a moment I am going to begin counting up from five to one, and when I get to one, you will be back in the present, fully alert and ready for the rest of your day... So counting now...		
	FIVE		
	FOUR... beginning to get feeling back into your hands and feet...		suggesting
	THREE shoulders moving... taking a deep breath... head moving...		pacing
	TWO and getting ready for a big stretch... and a smile, coming back to the present... eyelids fluttering... becoming aware of where you are...		pacing
	ONE: EYES OPEN, BACK AGAIN... fully alert...		
	Welcome back.		
	How do you feel?		

Permissive reorientation

The gentlest way to end the trance is to allow the client some quiet time to absorb what has been suggested during the session. Just tell the client that the session is over and they should consider what has been said, and can come back to full awareness when they are ready.

	Back to the present...		
	And so before coming back to full awareness....		presupposition
	take whatever time you need now... to consider those ideas... to allow your mind to examine things from every aspect... like a jeweller looking into the heart of a diamond...		
	and the lessons and possibilities... consider them deeply... absorb them deeply... into your very being... thinking about how best to apply them...		bind: best
	And when you have had enough time to process and learn from this session... then it is time to bring this session to a close, a comfortable close...	I	bind: time
	and you can start coming back to the present...		

	at whatever rate is right for you.		
	...so when you are fully prepared to... you can find yourself back in full awareness of the room around you, feeling refreshed... and knowing that you have finally settled something important.	I	

Some clients can take a very long time to come out of trance if you give them the option. You may have to hurry them along by using the count out procedure.

Post hypnotic suggestion reorientation

On coming out of trance the mind is still highly suggestible, so the Reorientation is a good time to slip in a few post hypnotic suggestions to reinforce the main points of the therapy.

	Back to the present...		
	And when you open your eyes you realise you are seeing things differently now, that things have changed... that you have changed... you are organised and focused and deeply confident.		
	And of all the changes you have made, I wonder what part you will enjoy the most?		
	And over the next few hours, and days and weeks you will become aware of changes in many things and that will let you know that the changes are working.		

Reorientation with option to sleep

If you want to give the client a recording of your script, it is nice to give them the option of listening to the recording before they go to sleep. This reorientation gives them the option of listening to it either during the day or last thing at night.

	Internal Visualisation and Reorientation		

So now [ClientName] just take a deep breath... and then let go... that's right.		
And another breath... and allow your mind to clear... that's good...		
And you can take as long as you want to come back to the present... and as you do... allow you mind to roam over your body... becoming aware of your muscles... your bones... your ligaments... your tendons... becoming aware of how they all fit together... become aware of any tension ... and just let that go now...	V	Give the client the option to do more work on anything that needs attention.
And allow yourself to feel that relaxation...feel your body making changes... things adjusting... flowing... learning... until you are ready to come back to the present... and then you have a choice... you can continue in this lovely relaxed feeling and just drift away or you can choose to come back and continue your normal activities...	V	Outline the options
So... when you are ready... to come back... you can count from five up to one... in your mind... and when you get to one... you will be back in the present... ready for the rest of your day and feeling refreshed and relaxed...		Option for day time use
Or you can decide to go into a deep refreshing sleep ... and just let go... by counting from ten down to one and becoming even more relaxed as each number goes by and you just drift away...		Option of using the script before bedtime
So when you are ready... you can start counting...		

Self Hypnosis

Self Hypnosis is simple and easy. This script shows you how to put yourself into trance, anywhere, anytime. You can use it to go to sleep, or you can use it to allow your mind to roam free. Self hypnosis can be very liberating. Many people feel a spirituality, a deep connection with something when they go into trance. Everyone's experience is unique. You can record the script and play it back to yourself, or you can study the structure and put yourself into trance by going over it in your mind. Both methods will work well. Eventually, after some practice, you will be able to slip into trance just by willing it.

Self Hypnosis script

Target	The induction - Relax the body...		Technique
	Take a deep breath... and let it go...		Slow down
	Now take another deep breath... and as you breathe out... just allow your whole body to relax and go limp....		the breathing
	and on the next breath... allow your eyes to close...		eye closure
	Now become aware of your body... notice if there is any tension anywhere... try shrugging your shoulders and letting them drop.... tense your legs and let them relax... roll your neck and let it relax... anywhere that is not loose... just tense and relax... until your whole body feels loose and heavy... and allow that feeling to continue.		Physical relaxation
	First Deepener - count down		
memory	And now I want you to imagine a line... or a chain or something like that... and I want you to imagine the numbers one to ten are spaced out along that line... and I want you to make the distance between number two and number three double the distance between one and two... and the distance between three	V	Always offer a choice of possible ways to form the line.

	and four is twice the distance of the distance between two and three... and so on... each number is separated by twice the distance of the previous number...	>	
Capability	And just imagine going along that line... from one to two... and two to three... and three to four... and the distances between each number gets longer and longer...		
	And as you think about that line... just imagine that in your mind you are sliding along the line... and as each number passes you get more relaxed... more at ease... and you can just feel yourself sinking ... down and down... and just keep doing that... and your breathing will get slower... and your pulse will get deeper....	I	
	And as each number comes along it gives you more time to relax... to let go...		
	and when you reach ten... you can just allow yourself to drift down and down some more... deeper and deeper... more and more relaxed... down and down...	>	
	allow that feeling to develop... you don't have to think... you don't have to do anything... all you have to do is to enjoy that lovely feeling of deep, deep relaxation...	I	
	and you can forget about everything... just allow your mind to drift away...	D	
	and if any day to day thoughts come into your mind... that' s OK... you can just stack them off to one side... and deal with them later... they're not important... nothing is important now...	D	
	... and each breath out is taking you deeper and deeper now... more and more relaxed...	>	breathing deepener
Second Deepener... Visualization			
	And now allow your mind to think of something you can write letters on... a blackboard or a big blue sky... whatever you want....		options
	imagine writing the letter 'A' ... and then just	V	

	imagine wiping away the letter 'A'...		
	and then imagine the letter 'B'... and then just imagine letter 'B' being wiped away... disappearing... in any way that makes sense to you...	V	
	and keep on thinking of the next letter... and as you wipe away the next letter... you can feel yourself... loosening... relaxing... getting more and more comfortable... letting go...	>	disappearing = relaxing
	and as each letter disappears you can become more and more relaxed... more at ease...	>	
	And you can continue putting the letters there... and fading out... and getting more comfortable...	>	who is 'fading'?
	and you relax more and more... until it becomes too much trouble to think of the next letter...	D	amnesia
	and then you can just relax completely...	I	'when' bind
	allow your mind to drift away... to a place where there is nothing to think about... nothing to worry you... relaxed and peaceful and calm...	V	Dissociation
Self Convincer			
	and as you drift deeper and deeper... become aware that one of your fingers or perhaps a thumb will feel the need to move... and that will be a signal to tell you that you are in trance... your body can just move on its own... without thought... just allow that to happen ... don't assist in any way... a finger or a thumb will want to move... and that will a signal that you have achieved the state of trance...	I	Give time - allow for those with a slow sub conscious
	It may be just a tiny tremor... and you may be surprised at what you experience...	V	Accept any signal
	and while you are in this state, notice everything about this state... and learn ... so you can recognise this state...		Anchor the feeling
	a state of unconscious awareness... of being in two minds... peaceful and relaxed.. and you can stay in this state as long as you like.	>	Reassurance

And in this state many things are possible...		
The visualisation - will be different each time		
Now... allow your mind to just wander... do not force anything... do not strive or try or do anything except accept what comes...		
an image or a memory or a feeling will form... just accept it... whatever comes is right... sometimes you will find a muscle moving... it can be anything... allow it to develop and observe...		
[Long Pause]		
[If nothing comes, that's OK. You have learned how to go into trance. That is enough. You should not expect to get something every time. Some days you just don't think of anything but relaxing and drifting. It is very therapeutic.]		
[If you get something, just regard it with curiosity. Become aware of what it does. Be an observer. Do not try to make sense of it, do not challenge it. Nothing in your own mind can ever harm you. It may just fade, it may transform into something else. There are no rules. What you experiencing is a metaphoric representation of what is going on in your own subconscious mind. Sometimes you will recognise the metaphor, sometimes not.]		
[If you learn the principles of Clean Language you can begin to interact with the image or symbol or feeling or whatever comes up. Otherwise just treat the whole thing as if it was a dream and allow it to develop in its own way.]		
[The whole dreamy, drifty thing will go on for some time and you may get more than one. Seeing parts of faces is very common. It doesn't mean anything.]		
And then, when you are ready... you can begin to return from trance...		

The Reorientation		
And so before coming back to full awareness....		presupposition
take whatever time you need now... to consider those ideas... those images... to allow your mind to examine things from every aspect... like a jeweller looking into the heart of a diamond...		
and the lessons and possibilities... consider them deeply... absorb them deeply... into your very being... thinking about how best to apply them...		bind: best
And when you have had enough time to process and learn from this session... then it is time to bring this session to a close, a comfortable close...	I	bind: time
and you can start coming back to the present... at whatever rate is right for you.		
So take as long as you like to consider these things...		
And when you are ready ... you can come back to the present... refreshed and awake and alert and ready for the rest of your day.		

David Mason   www.key-hypnosis.com © 2008

Self hypnosis sleep induction

Self hypnosis is a great way to relax into sleep. All you have to do is to relax your body, then focus on your breathing, and finally allow your mind to drift away.

This hypnotic relaxation script is easy to learn and easy to do. If you follow this self hypnosis script you can train your unconscious mind to learn to go into trance on a signal, and then to go into sleep from trance.

	So settle back now, get comfortable... and close your eyes....	
	Now take a deep breath, and hold it... and ... just let it all go... ahhhh...That's good...	Start releasing tension
	When you are ready... take another deep breath..... and as you do... lift your shoulders up... and as you breath out... let them slump down and relax.	Let go muscle tension
	Now lift your arms slightly... and on the next breath out... let them drop back naturally... and relax your whole body	Let go muscle tension
	Now imagine what it would be like if your arms and legs have become so heavy ... that you just could not move them... that they felt as if they were made of lead...	D Dissociation
	...and just allow that heaviness to grow	
	... and now I would like you to focus on your breathing... just become aware of the gentle in and out of your breath...	D Dissociation
	And as you think about your breathing... with each breath out... just allow your body to relax more...	I Dissociation
	and with each breath out... say to yourself... in your mind...quietly... *Relaxing now*...	
	and with each breath in... say to yourself... *calm and easy*...	Meditation
	Continue breathing gently... in and out... allow the natural pattern of breathing to take over...	Affirmation Meditation
	and when you breath in... think... *Calm and easy*	D Deepening

	and when you breath out... think... *'Relaxing now'*...		Deepening
	and continue that way... breathing gently... enjoying the feelings... letting go...	I	
	and your mind might drift here and there... and that's OK... and if any day to day thoughts come into your mind you can just stack them off in a corner somewhere... they're not important now... just allow the breathing to continue... calm and easy... relaxing it all away...	I	Reassurance
Capability	it's easy to learn to relax like this...		
	Focusing on your breathing... with each breath out... your body relaxes more...	I	Dissociation
	and with each breath out... saying to yourself... *'Relaxing now'*...		
	and each breath in.... . *'calm and easy'*...		Meditation
	and feel your body relaxing... easing... more and more... going down and down....		
	and now you allow your mind to drift away... utterly relaxed... feel your body sinking down now... and forget about everything...	D	

David Mason   www.key-hypnosis.com © 2011

Printed in Great Britain
by Amazon.co.uk, Ltd.,
Marston Gate.